Culinary Arts Institute®

GREEK
COOKBOOK

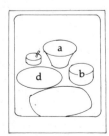

Featured in cover photo:
a. **Tossed Salad and Vinegar and Oil Dressing with Tomato, 51**
b. **Yialandji Dolmathes, 17**
c. **Broiled Chicken in Lemon Juice and Oregano, 72**
d. **Kourambiethes, 91**

GREEK

GREEK COOKBOOK

Margot Kopsidas Phillips and
the Culinary Arts Institute staff:

Helen Geist: Director
Sherrill Weary: Editor • Joy Taylor: Assistant Editor
Edward Finnegan: Executive Editor • Charles Bozett: Art Director
Susan Bradley: Editorial Assistant • Ivanka Simatic: Recipe Tester
Malinda Miller: Copy Editor

Book designed and coordinated by Charles Bozett

Illustrations by George Suyeoka

Photographs by Zdenek Pivecka

Adventures in Cooking SERIES

COOKBOOK

Culinary Arts Institute®
A DIVISION OF DELAIR PUBLISHING COMPANY

ISBN: 0-8326-0611-1
Library of Congress Catalog Card
Number: 79-51590

CONTENTS

CONTENTS

GREEK CUISINE

From the beginning, Greeks have always taken food seriously. Among ancient Greeks, there was a rule that once you had eaten at a man's table you ought not do him any harm, and he, too, had to treat you with full courtesy. Those who failed to do this brought on themselves the wrath of the gods.

The punishment of a man named Tantalus, who was made forever thirsty in the midst of drink, and hungry in the midst of food, was the result of his undesirable behavior at a banquet.

Around A.D. 230, Athenaeus, a compiler of writings on food and eating of the preceding five hundred years, tells of a rich epicure who spent most of his life and fortune seeking culinary delights. The epicure went so far as to travel from his home to the African coast because he had heard the crayfish found there surpassed those at home. His trip was in vain. Without ever going ashore, he determined that the African crayfish were no better than those at home. Having spent most of his fortune seeking such pleasures, and fearful that he would starve to death, he committed suicide after a long and lavish banquet.

The ancient Greeks apparently did not concern themselves with calories. At banquets, hosts served chickens, geese, ducks, doves, and hares, as well as whole pigs whose stuffing included thrushes, eggs, oysters, and scallops. The menu further included roast boar and kid, tripe, ham with mustard, roast fish, wine, bread, cheese cake, shrimp, olives, dolmathes, and chestnuts. Roast grasshopper, marinated octopus, oysters, caviar, and pâté of goose liver were also served.

No one was expected to eat everything offered. Slaves accompanied their masters to carry home the leftovers and the gold and silver trays on which the food had been served.

Cooking was so esteemed that the creation of a new recipe

equaled the importance of a new poem. Laws were extended to protect special recipes, allowing their creators full copyright for one year.

Modern Greek food has been profoundly affected by the Greek church, and by the Turks who ruled Greece for four centuries after Constantinople fell to them in 1453. By the time Greece regained its independence in the mid-nineteenth century, the Greek cuisine included Turkish coffee, loukoumia, moussaka, and halvah. Only the seven Ionian Islands, under the Venetian protectorate, escaped Turkish influence.

That the church was a powerful force in Greek life has been chronicled by writers who give details of the faithful routinely participating in church festivals, fasting preceding certain religious holy days, cooking the Paschal lamb, and taking food and drink to church for blessing.

The religious season before, during, and after Easter is replete with caveats concerning food.

The season begins with Apokria, a period of masquerading and merrymaking. The word "apokria" means "from meat." The forty-day Lenten period which follows is one of austere fasting. The first day is a national holiday and is called Kathary-Deftera, "Clean Monday." Families go to the country for picnics, where they eat sea urchins, pickles, and lagana, a bread, as well as other special foods. All during Lent neither meat, nor animal products, nor fish with blood may be eaten.

Resurrection services are held the Saturday night before Easter. At midnight churches are plunged into darkness. The priest emerges from the sanctuary holding lighted tapers and chanting, "Come, receive the Light." The fast is broken after the services when the parishioners eat Easter eggs. At home, mayeritsa, koulourakia, and more eggs await them.

Following the Agape (Love) services, which are held Sunday afternoon, everyone sits down to a feast that includes baby lamb, wine, tsoureki, and koulourakia before the dancing begins. It is truly a happy occasion.

Ordinarily, the gulf is vast between the well-heeled Athenian and the poor peasant in terms of the food available to each. The rich city dweller may select foods of the world such as Tournedos, Roz Bif, Salata Roseiki, ginger beer, milk shakes, and hamburgers. This is due, in part, to the sophisticated tastes and education of the urbanites and to the equipment available with which to prepare and store the foods. Many cultures influenced Greece. Culinary imports from Slavs, French, Venetians, and, more recently, the British and Americans continue to turn up on menus.

The diet of peasants is frugal, consisting mostly of yogurt, legumes, soups, fresh olive oil, bread, cheese, and wine. Meat and fish are eaten less frequently.

The countryside of Greece is rich with olive groves. The silver trees with their gnarled trunks are renowned for their natural beauty. Their fruit produces a sweet, light-colored oil which has never been captured in the canning process.

Most Greek recipes were developed in village kitchens which had no electricity or running water. Yet, the cooks produced tasty, elaborate foods. Peasant resourcefulness de-

veloped such kitchen aids as two forks with their tines laced together to fashion a primitive egg beater that worked efficiently enough to bring a dozen egg whites to stiff peaks.

Besides no electricity or running water, there were also no cookbooks. Among Greeks, the art of cooking is part of the oral tradition and cultural practice. Greek cooks have an innate feel for food. This assumption is fostered in girls as soon as they are old enough to help with simple chores. Learning through practical experience, their training includes developing an ability to discern how much of an ingredient is required, when a dish is cooked, and when a dough is ready for forming.

This training develops an intuitive sense so that the cooks, without recipes, have a feel for how many eggs a dough needs to make a certain kind of cake; or how much spice to add for a given flavor; or what kinds of vegetables complement each other in a stew.

Recipes in this book are family recipes that have been passed down from one generation to the next. They have been adjusted so that exact proportions and directions are given.

Modern Greeks, continuing to follow the edict of hospitality ordained by Zeus, extend their hospitality with a warm toast to their guests: "Oti epythymas, file"—which translates to, "Whatever you wish, my friend."

Kaly orexi! Good appetite!

GLOSSARY

analogos (ah-NAH-loh-gohs)—in proportion, to taste

angourodomatosalata (ahn-goo-roh-doh-mah-toh-sah-LAH-tah)—cucumber and tomato salad

anitho (AH-nee-thoh)—dill

arni (ahr-NEE)—lamb; traditional meat, usually eaten before lamb is one year old; it is a menu highlight at Eastertime and on special occasions

arni me antithia avgolemono (ahr-nee meh ahn-DEE-theea ahv-goh-LEH-moh-noh)—lamb with endive avgolemono

astakos (ah-stah-KOHS)—lobster

avgo (ahv-GOH)—egg

avgolemono (ahv-goh-LEH-moh-noh)—egg and lemon sauce

bakaliaro (bah-kah-lee-AH-roh)—codfish

baklava (bah-klah-VAH)—dessert made of filo, nuts, and topped with a sugar syrup

bamies (BAH-mee-ehs)—okra

bamies giahni me lathi (BAH-mee-ehs ghyah-NEE meh LAH-thee)—okra with tomatoes

béchamel sauce (besh-ah-MEL)—a creamy white sauce

briki (BREE-kee)—coffee pot

Copenhai (ko-pen-AAGH-ee)—dessert with a cakelike base layered with almonds, created in 1863 by a Greek chef in honor of the Dane, King George I, upon his coronation as king of Greece

diples (THEE-plehs)—a dessert fried in hot oil

dolmathes (dol-MAH-thes)—stuffed grapevine leaves

faki (fah-KEE)—lentils

feta (FEH-tah)—flaky, white cheese made from goat's milk, stored in brine

filo (FEE-loh)—leaf-thin sheets of dough, sometimes homemade, more frequently commercially made, used for appetizers such as tyropites, entrées such as kefalonian meat pie, vegetable dishes like spanakopeta and desserts like baklava. The plural of filo is fila.

galatobouriko (gah-lah-tah-BOO-ree-koh)—dessert made of filo and a custard filling of semolina, milk, and eggs drenched in a syrup

garithes (gah-RI-thehs)—shrimp

garyfallo (gah-REE-fah-loh)—clove

ghiristra (ghee-RYH-strah)—spatula

giahni (ghyah-NEE)—stew

glikaniso (glee-KAH-nee-soh)—anise

hilopites (hee-loh-PEEH-tes)—homemade noodles, literally "a thousand noodles"

hirono (hee-roh-NOH)—pork; also known as **gourouni** (ghooh-ROOH-nee)

honi (hon-NEE)—funnel

hortarika (hor-tah-ree-KAH)—vegetables

kafes (kah-FES)—coffee

kalamaria (kah-lah-MAH-ree-ah)—squid

kaly orexi (kah-LEE OH-re-ksee)—good appetite

kanella (kah-NEH-lah)—cinnamon

karvoudizmena (kahr-voo-deez-MEH-nah)—roasted

kasseri (kah-SEH-ree)—a rich, mellow cheese, generally served in slices; may be grated

kastana (KAH-stah-nah)—chestnuts

kataifi (kah-tah-EE-fee)—dessert made of shredded wheat, filled with nuts, and moistened with a sugar syrup

kazani (kah-ZAH-nee)—large pot

kefalotyri (keh-fah-loh-TEE-ree)—very hard, salty, light yellow cheese; excellent for grating

keftethes (kehf-TEH-thes)—meatballs

kimino (KEE-mee-noh)—cumin

koliandro (koh-lee-AHN-droh)—coriander

kolyva (KOH-lee-vah)—boiled wheat mixed with nuts, currants, spices, and sesame seed, and decorated with confectioners' sugar; prepared for distribution in small bags after services memorializing someone who has died

koskino (KOHS-kee-noh)—a sifter with horsehair or copper mesh

kotopoulo (koh-TOH-poo-loh)—chicken

koukounaria (koo-koo-NAH-ree-ah)—pine nuts, also known by their Italian name, pignolia

koulourakia (koo-loo-RAH-kee-ah)—butter biscuits that are fairly hard and not too sweet; served traditionally at Eastertime, a staple in Greek homes

koutala (koo-TAH-lah)—ladle

krasi (krah-SEE)—wine

kreas moshariou (KREH-ahs mohs-hah-REE-oo)—veal; the most tender meat comes from milkfed calves, 2 to 3 months old

ksistros (KSEE-strohs)—a metal grater

ksithi (KSEE-thee)—vinegar

Lambropsomo (lahm-BROH-psoh-moh)—Greek Easter Bread

lathi (LAH-thee)—olive oil

lemoni (leh-MOH-nee)—lemon

loukanika (loo-KAH-nee-kah)—sausage

Magyrevo (mah-ghee-REH-voh)—I am cooking

maitanos (ma-ee-dah-NOHS)—parsley

mastiha (mah-STEE-ha)—mastic; a gum that is pulverized and used in breads, cookies, and in a liqueur

Mavrodaphne (mah-vroh-DAF-nee)—sweet, dessert wine

mayoneza (mah-ghyoh-NEH-za)—mayonnaise

melitzanes tyganites (meh-lee-tzah-nes tee-ghah-nee-TES)—fried eggplant

mezethakia (meh-zeh-THAH-kee-ah)—a collection of appetizers

mia houfta (mee-ah HOOHF-tah)—one handful

mizithra (mee-ZEE-thra)—semihard and salted cheese; served in slices or grated. **Soft mizithra**—unsalted cheese made from whey after curd is removed from milk (similar to ricotta cheese)

moskokaryon (mohs-koh-KAH-ree-ohn)—nutmeg

neistisimo fahgyto (nee-STEE-see-moh fah-ghee-TOH)—fasting food usually eaten during Lent that is devoid of all animal products and which, during Holy Week, is cooked without olive oil

ohso hryazete (OH-soh hree-AH-zeh-teh)—as much as needed

oktapodi (ohk-tah-POH-thee)—octopus

pahos (PAH-hos)—fat

parakalo (pah-rah-kah-LOH)—please

Pasha (PAH-sghah)—Easter

paximathia (pah-ksee-MAH-thee-ah)—rusks, another staple in Greek homes. They are always served following a meal of fish and salad with coffee after a funeral in the deceased person's home

pilafi (pee-LAH-fee)—a kind of cooked rice

pligouri (plee-GOOH-ree)—cracked wheat pilafi

portokali (por-toh-KAH-lee)—orange

patates me avga tyganita (pah-TAH-tehs meh ahv-GHA tee-gha-nee-TAH)—fried potatoes and scrambled eggs

poto (poh-TOH)—drink

prassa vrasta (prah-SAH vrah-STAH)—braised leeks

Prosphoron (PROHS-foh-ron)—the offering bread baked by Greek women who offer the bread to their churches where, during the Divine Liturgy, the priests bless and cut it. Part of the loaf serves as the Host during the service. (More information on page 93.)

proyno (proh-ee-NOH)—breakfast

prozymi (proh-ZEE-mee)—yeast

psari (PSA-ree)—fish

psito (psee-TOH)—roast

psomi (pso-MEE)—bread

revithia (reh-VEE-thee-ah)—chickpeas

rigani (REE-gah-nee)—oregano

saganaki (sah-gah-NAH-kee)—fried cheese

saltsa (SAHL-tsah)—sauce or gravy

saltsa yaourti yia frouta (SAHL-tsa yhea-OOR-ti yeea FROO-tah)—yogurt sauce for fruit

semolina (seh-moh-LEE-nah)—coarsely ground wheat meal

sfragitha (sfrah-GEE-thah)—seal, used during the preparation of the church bread, Prosphoron

skhara (SKAH-rah)—grill for broiling

skorthalia (skor-thah-LEEA)—garlic sauce

skortho (SKOHR-thoh)—garlic

soupa (SOO-pah)—soup

soupa trahana avgolemono (SOO-pah trah-hah-NAH ahv-gho-LEH-moh-noh)—egg and lemon soup with sour-dough noodles

souvles (SOO-vlehs)—skewers

spanakopeta (spah-nah-KOH-pee-tah)—pastry with filo, spinach, and cheese

spanakorizo (spah-nah-KOH-ree-zoh)—spinach with rice

stifatho (stee-FAH-thoh)—stew in which the principal vegetable is baby onions

tapsi (tahp-SEE)—baking pan

thafni (THAF-nee)—bay leaves

thendrolivano (then-droh-LEE-vah-noh)—rosemary

Then thelo, efharisto (thehn THE-loh ef-hah-ree-STOH)—I don't want any, thank you

thiosmo (thee-OHS-moh)—mint

thymari (thee-MAH-ree)—thyme

trahana (trah-hah-NAH)—noodle usually made with yogurt or buttermilk

trigona (TREE-goh-nah)—nut-filled filo folded in triangles

tsoukali (tsoo-KAH-lee)—pot

tygani (tee-GAH-nee)—frying pan

tyri (tee-REE)—cheese

tyrobiskota (tee-roh-bis-KOH-tah)—crisp cheese crackers

vasiliko (vah-see-lee-KOH)—basil

Vasilopita (vah-see-LOH-pee-tah)—New Year's Day bread, named in honor of St. Basil, Bishop of Caesarea in Cappadocia in A.D. 370, whose nameday is celebrated on January 1.

vothinon kreas (voh-thee-NOHN KREH-ahs)—meat from cattle (beef)

voutero (VOO-tee-roh)—butter

yevma (YEHV-mah)—dinner

Yne nostimo (EE-neh NOH-stee-moh)—It is tasty

zestos (zeh-STOHS)—hot

zoumi (zooh-MEE)—juice, liquid

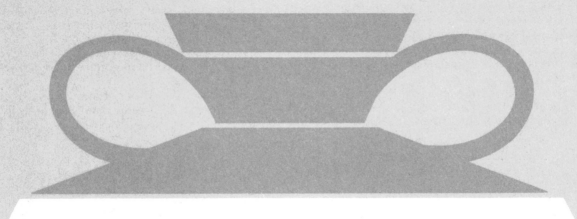

HORS D' OEUVRES

Guests are welcomed in Greek homes with "Kalos ylthes," (food, wine)—and hors d'oeuvres. The food may vary from a simple boiled potato and a little homemade wine in the home of a poor peasant to a table spread lavishly with a variety of foods.

Usually served in bite-size portions and arranged on platters with the care of an artist doing a still life, the hors d'oeuvres offered during an afternoon or evening visit may include Dolmathes, Taramosalata, Splinandero, octopus, cheeses, and cucumber and tomato slices.

In the morning, a host may say "Kalos ylthes" with Paximathia, Koulourakia, some cheese, and hardboiled eggs.

Some of the many foods offered as hors d'oeuvres can, in larger portions, be meals in themselves.

Fried Cheese *(Saganaki)*

Kefalotyri or kasseri cheese, sliced lengthwise in ¼-inch-thick wedges (about 1 pound for 4 people)
2 egg yolks mixed with 2 tablespoons water
Flour
Olive oil
2 lemons, cut in quarters

1. Dip cheese slices into egg-yolk mixture, then into flour, coating each side evenly. Shake off excess flour.
2. In a 10-inch skillet, heat a ¼-inch layer of olive oil. When the oil begins to smoke, add the cheese. Fry first on one side, then on the other.
3. Remove from skillet and squeeze some lemon juice on each slice. Serve immediately. Allow 2 slices of Saganaki for each person.

Crisp Cheese Crackers *(Tyrobiskota)*

¼ cup sesame seed
2 cups all-purpose flour
Salt (optional)
½ teaspoon ground red pepper
1½ cups grated kefalotyri cheese
¾ cup butter, softened
¼ cup olive oil
2 egg yolks, beaten, for brushing
Sesame seed

1. Combine ¼ cup sesame seed, flour, salt, red pepper, and cheese. Work in butter and oil, using hands. Mix until dough holds together.
2. Roll dough out on lightly floured board. Cut into small diamond shapes. Transfer to cookie sheets. Brush with egg yolks and sprinkle with sesame seed.
3. Bake at 350°F about 12 minutes, or until golden.

About 3 dozen

Marrow Canapés

8 large marrow bones, cut in 2-inch pieces
Salted water
½ cup butter
1 loaf cocktail-size black bread, cut in thick slices
¼ cup minced parsley
Ground red pepper

1. Using a thin sharp knife, loosen marrow from bones and remove. Soak marrow in salted water for 24 hours. Drain.
2. Cut marrow into ½-inch-thick rounds and poach in simmering water until tender (2 to 3 minutes). Remove with a slotted spoon. Drain on paper towels.
3. Melt butter in a skillet. Fry slices of bread on both sides.
4. Spread slices with marrow. Sprinkle with parsley and red pepper.
5. Place under broiler for a moment. Serve hot.

12 to 15 pieces

Cocktail Meatballs *(Keftethes)*

1 large onion, minced
2 tablespoons olive oil
1½ pounds freshly ground round steak (half each of lamb and veal)
3 tablespoons cracker meal
2 cups firm-type bread, crusts removed
2 eggs
6 tablespoons chopped parsley
2 teaspoons oregano, crushed
1½ teaspoons mint
2 tablespoons vinegar
Salt and pepper to taste
Flour
Olive or corn oil for deep frying heated to 365°F

1. Brown half of onion in 2 tablespoons oil in a small frying pan. Mix with the uncooked onion and add to meat in a large bowl. Add the remaining ingredients except flour and oil. Toss lightly with two forks to mix thoroughly.
2. Dust hands with flour. Roll a small amount of meat at a time between palms, shaping into a ball.
3. To heated fat in deep fryer, add the meatballs a layer at a time. Fry until browned on all sides (about 12 minutes). Serve hot.

30 to 40 meatballs

Eggplant Appetizer *(Salata Melitzana)*

1 large eggplant
1 medium onion, minced
1 garlic clove, crushed in a garlic press
1 teaspoon chopped parsley
½ teaspoon freshly dried mint
½ cup olive oil
1 tablespoon wine vinegar (or more to taste)
Juice of 1 large lemon
Salt and pepper to taste

1. To prepare eggplant, place in a baking pan and prick top in four or five places with a fork.
2. Bake at 350°F about 45 minutes, or until skin is wrinkled and the surface is soft.
3. Cool eggplant slightly and cut in half. Scoop out the flesh and place in a blender. Add onion, garlic, parsley, and mint. Blend until well mixed.
4. Combine olive oil, vinegar, and lemon juice. Add to the eggplant mixture and blend well. Season with salt and pepper.
5. Chill. Serve with **toasted French** or **pita bread.** May also be used as a dip for fresh vegetables, or served separately as a first course.

About 4 cups

Olive Canapés

1 pound Greek olives, pitted
2 tablespoons olive oil
4 hard-cooked eggs, mashed
Pinch dry mustard
1 clove garlic, crushed in a garlic press
Pepper to taste
Egg yolks, hard-cooked and chopped for garnish
Scallions (green part), minced for garnish

1. Put olives and olive oil into a blender; purée. Blend in remaining ingredients except yolks and scallions.
2. Serve on **crackers,** or mound in a dish and serve crackers separately. Garnish with egg yolks and scallions.

1 cup

Yogurt Dip

2 cups plain yogurt
1 garlic clove, crushed in a garlic press
1 teaspoon dill
1 teaspoon mint
1 teaspoon wine vinegar

1. Combine all ingredients. Chill.
2. Serve with **toasted pita bread** or as a dip for **fresh vegetables.** May also be served as an accompaniment to roast meats or with pilaf.

2 cups

Red Caviar Dip *(Taramosalata)*

1 jar (4 ounces) tarama (fish roe)
10 slices firm-type whole wheat bread, crusts removed
Water
1 medium onion, minced
2 cups olive oil
Juice of 2 or 3 lemons

1. Beat tarama in a mixer for 5 minutes at medium speed.
2. Sprinkle bread lightly with water and squeeze very dry. Add bread, slice by slice, to tarama, beating after each addition. Add onion and beat. Slowly pour in olive oil, alternating with lemon juice to taste. Beat until fluffy. Refrigerate.
3. Serve with **crackers** or small pieces of crusty **Greek bread.**

5 cups

Note: Store in the refrigerator no longer than a week.

Salami Cornucopias

1 package (8 ounces) cream cheese
¼ cup grated kefalotyri cheese
¼ teaspoon pepper
Pinch dry mustard
½ pound salami, sliced very thin

1. Combine cheeses, pepper, and mustard. Beat well.
2. With a small knife or spoon, put a teaspoon of the mixture at the bottom of a salami slice.
3. Roll over to form a cornucopia. Secure with a wooden pick.

18 to 20 cornucopias

Kalamata Olives

2 pounds kalamata olives preserved in brine
¾ cup wine vinegar
¼ cup olive oil

1. Rinse olives in ½ cup wine vinegar. Drain.
2. Pour olive oil and remaining vinegar in a glass jar. Add the olives. Shake well. Store in refrigerator until ready to serve.

Baked Clams Oregano

12 clams
3 tablespoons minced onion
Salt and pepper to taste
1 teaspoon oregano
1 teaspoon minced parsley
5 tablespoons olive oil
Juice of 1 lemon

1. Open clams. Arrange side by side in a small baking dish.
2. Combine onion, salt, pepper, oregano, parsley, olive oil, and lemon juice. Spoon on clam meat.
3. Bake at 325°F about 7 minutes, or until clams curl slightly at the edges.

3 servings

These are typical ingredients for Greek cooking

Yialandji Dolmathes

1 jar (32 ounces) grapevine leaves
1 quart water
½ cup olive oil
3 medium onions, finely chopped
1½ cups long-grain rice
Juice of 2 lemons
2 tablespoons pine nuts
1 tablespoon dried black currants
2 teaspoons dill
2 teaspoons mint
¼ cup minced parsley
Salt and pepper to taste
Water (about 1 cup)
Olive oil (about 1 cup)

1. To prepare grapevine leaves, rinse leaves thoroughly in cold running water to remove brine.
2. Bring 1 quart water to a boil. Add leaves and parboil 3 minutes. Drain.
3. Select 4 or 5 heavy leaves and line bottom of a medium-size Dutch oven. Set aside.
4. To prepare filling, heat ½ cup olive oil in a medium skillet. Add onion and cook until translucent. Remove with a slotted spoon.
5. In a saucepan, parboil rice in 1 cup water until liquid is absorbed.
6. Combine rice, onion, lemon juice, pine nuts, currants, dill, mint, and parsley. Season with salt and pepper. Cool.
7. To fill grapevine leaves, place a leaf on a working surface, rough side up with stem pointing toward you. Place about a teaspoon of the rice mixture at the base of the leaf. Lift the bottom sides of the leaf up onto the filling. Fold both the right and left sides of the leaf over the filling. Roll up, tucking the edges in.
8. Place the stuffed grape leaves (dolmathes) side by side in the Dutch oven to cover the bottom. Put a second layer on top of the first one. Continue to do this until all the stuffed leaves have been put in.
9. Add water and olive oil to cover. Place an inverted plate on the dolmathes. Bring to boiling. Cover Dutch oven, lower heat, and simmer 1 hour. Taste a dolma to see if rice is tender. If necessary, continue cooking.
10. Cool dolmathes in liquid. Remove carefully with a spoon. Chill in refrigerator 24 hours before serving. Serve cold.

About 50 dolmathes

Note: Dolmathes will keep 10 days in the refrigerator.

Sesame Seed Dip (Tahi)

½ cup tahini (sesame seed paste)
2 tablespoons olive oil (or more to taste)
¾ cup water
Juice of 1 lemon
2 garlic cloves, crushed in a garlic press
½ cup walnuts
Salt and pepper to taste
¼ cup sesame seed, toasted

1. In a blender, combine all the ingredients except sesame seed until smooth and milky white in color. Refrigerate.
2. Garnish with sesame seed. Serve with **crackers** or as a vegetable dip.

About 1 ¾ cups

Anchovy Fillets

½ pound anchovy fillets
    preserved in salt
Wine vinegar (2 or more cups)
2 tablespoons olive oil

1. Separate fillets. Scrape scales and as much of the salt as possible from each fillet.
2. Soak in wine vinegar 5 to 10 minutes, changing as often as necessary until the vinegar remains clear.
3. Drain fillets on paper towels.
4. Arrange fillets on a serving platter. Drizzle with 1 tablespoon fresh vinegar and the olive oil.
5. Serve as an hors d'oeuvre or in anchovy salad.

Fried Calf, Lamb, or Chicken Livers *(Sikotakia Tyganita)*

1 pound livers, cut in small
    pieces (do not cut chicken
    livers)
1½ cups flour, seasoned with
    pepper for dredging
Olive oil for frying
2 lemons, quartered
Salt to taste

1. Rinse livers in cool water. Drain on absorbent paper.
2. Dip livers in flour. Shake off excess.
3. In a deep skillet, heat olive oil to smoking. Brown livers on both sides over medium heat.
4. Squeeze lemon juice on each piece. Season with salt. Serve at once.

4 servings

Barbecued Lamb Innards *(Splinandero Karsaniko)*

1 large intestine
Innards (heart, liver, kidneys,
    lungs, and sweetbreads) from
    a milk-fed calf
Salt to taste
1 tablespoon vinegar
¾ cup olive oil
Juice of 2 to 3 lemons
2 garlic cloves, crushed in a
    garlic press
2 teaspoons pepper
2 teaspoons oregano
1 teaspoon thyme
2 lamb casings, washed and
    drained
Pepper to taste

1. Rinse intestine in lukewarm water. Using a long spit, turn inside out. Rub salt over surface. Wash thoroughly in lots of lukewarm water.
2. Put innards in a large bowl. Cover with lukewarm water. Add salt and vinegar. Let stand ½ hour. Drain. Discard membranes and connective tissues. Cut into pieces.
3. Combine olive oil, lemon juice, garlic, 2 teaspoons pepper, oregano, and thyme. Add innards. Marinate in refrigerator 4 to 6 hours, turning occasionally.
4. Drain innards, reserving marinade. Knot one end of casing, then stuff with innards and knot other end.
5. Put a skewer beside the filled casing (splinandero). Tie the splinandero to the skewer with the empty casing by turning the casing around the length of the skewer.
6. Charcoal-broil over embers heated until they are white, turning about every 10 minutes and brushing frequently with the marinade. Cook until tender (about 2½ hours). Remove from spit. Cut into 2-inch pieces. Sprinkle with pepper. Serve hot.

10 to 20 pieces

SOUPS

Soups have an integral place in Greek culture as well as in its cuisine. Fassoulatha and Faki, made without animal products, are mainstays of meals during periods of fasting.

Mayeritsa, a delicious and unusual combination of ground lamb innards and egg and lemon sauce flavored with fresh dill, has been the soup with which Greek Orthodox have, for centuries, begun their Easter celebration.

Some soups, such as Soupa Aravanaiko, are one-dish meals which the housewives of Karia and Lef-kas have served their families for generations.

The famous Avgolemono Soupa has two little-known variations: Soupa Trahana, to which home-made sourdough noodles are added to create a velvety soup perfect for a cold evening; and Soupa Xerokosta, made with milk and cream, that is a favorite of the Athenian élite.

Beef Stock

6 to 8 pounds beef soup bones
Salt to taste
2 large onions, peeled and left whole
10 peppercorns
2 whole allspice
2 carrots, scraped
4 parsley sprigs
2 bay leaves
2 celery stalks
Water to cover bones

1. Combine all ingredients in a 12-quart saucepot. Bring to boiling, lower heat, and simmer 10 to 12 hours, skimming off foam from top.
2. Strain. Discard solids. Cool. Skim off fat. Taste for salt.

7 to 8 quarts

Creamed Avgolemono Soup *(Soupa Xerokosta Avgolemono)*

1 cup butter, softened
6 tablespoons flour
2 cups milk, scalded
2 cups cream, scalded
1½ quarts homemade chicken stock, strained
2 cups cooked rice
4 egg yolks
Juice of 3 lemons
1 lemon, thinly sliced for garnish

1. Beat butter in a small bowl. Beating constantly, slowly add flour.
2. Combine butter mixture with scalded milk and cream in a soup pot. Cook over medium heat, stirring frequently, until boiling. Reduce heat at once.
3. Pour in stock and add rice. Simmer 30 minutes, skimming off fat.
4. Beat egg yolks in a large bowl until fluffy. Pour in lemon juice a little at a time, while beating. Add 2 cups hot stock, a tablespoon at a time, while beating.
5. Pour stock mixture into soup. Heat, but do not boil. Garnish with sliced lemon.

6 servings

Egg and Lemon Soup *(Avgolemono Soupa)*

1½ quarts chicken stock
    (homemade or canned)
1½ cups uncooked parboiled rice
  1 whole egg
  3 egg yolks
    Juice of 2 lemons
    Salt and pepper to taste

1. Heat stock in a saucepan. Add rice and simmer, covered, until tender (about 20 minutes).
2. Beat egg and yolks until light. Beating constantly, slowly add lemon juice.
3. Measure 2 cups hot chicken stock and add, tablespoon by tablespoon, to egg mixture, beating constantly to prevent curdling. Add this mixture to the remaining hot chicken stock with rice. Season with salt and pepper.
4. Serve at once.

6 servings

Egg and Lemon Soup with Sour-Dough Noodles
(Trahana Avgolemono)

1½ quarts chicken broth
  1 cup trahana (see Note)
    Salt and pepper to taste
  2 eggs, separated
    Juice of 2 lemons

1. Bring broth to boiling; boil 6 minutes. Add trahana, salt, and pepper. Simmer covered 10 minutes.
2. In a small bowl, using a wire whisk, beat egg whites until frothy. In another bowl, beat egg yolks. Combine. Slowly beat in lemon juice, then 1 cup hot broth. Add to soup. Serve immediately.

About 2½ cups

Note: There are three varieties of trahana dough—sour, sweet, sweet-sour. It may be made at home (see recipe for Sweet-Sour Trahana and variations) or purchased at a Greek grocery store.

Sweet-Sour Trahana

  2 eggs, slightly beaten
 ½ cup plain yogurt
 ½ cup milk
  1 teaspoon salt
1½ cups all-purpose flour
    Semolina (about 1½ cups)

1. Blend eggs, yogurt, milk, and salt. Add flour and semolina, a little at a time, to form a stiff dough.
2. Knead for about 5 minutes (dough will be very sticky). Divide into small portions. Roll with hands into balls. Place on a clean cloth.
3. Flatten each piece as thin as possible. Let dry undisturbed on trivets at least 12 hours.
4. Cut into small pieces. Turn pieces over and continue drying for another 12 hours or more.
5. When completely dry, mash into crumbs with rolling pin. Spread on a baking sheet.
6. Bake at 200°F for 2 hours.

Note: The weather affects the drying of the trahana. When it is humid, allow more time for drying. Homemade trahana is far superior to the commercially made product. Store in an airtight jar indefinitely.

Sweet Trahana: Follow recipe for Sweet-Sour Trahana; omit yogurt and increase milk to 1 cup.

Sour Trahana: Follow recipe for Sweet-Sour Trahana; omit milk and increase yogurt to 1 cup.

Bean Soup *(Fassoulatha)*

1 cup large dried white beans
2 quarts water
1 cup sliced celery (½-inch pieces)
2 cups chopped onion
4 medium carrots, cut in ½-inch slices
½ cup chopped parsley
1 tablespoon tomato paste
1 cup olive oil
1 tablespoon oregano, crushed
3 tablespoons wine vinegar

Bring beans to a boil in the water. Reduce heat and simmer 1 hour. Add remaining ingredients. Simmer 2 hours more. Add **salt** and **pepper** to taste. Serve with **toasted bread.**

6 to 8 servings

Lentil Soup *(Faki)*

1 package (16 ounces) dried lentils
2 quarts water
½ cup olive oil
1 cup chopped celery
½ cup grated carrot
1 onion, quartered
1 tablespoon tomato paste
3 garlic cloves, peeled
2 bay leaves
Salt and pepper to taste
Vinegar

1. Rinse lentils several times. Drain.
2. In a kettle, put lentils, water, olive oil, celery, carrot, onion, tomato paste, garlic, bay leaves, salt, and pepper. Bring to a boil. Reduce heat and simmer covered 2 hours. Adjust salt and pepper.
3. Serve with a cruet of vinegar.

6 to 8 servings

Soupa Aravanaiko

This soup is a delicious main course with homemade bread on a cold night.

3 quarts beef stock
3 pounds lean beef, cut in 2½-inch squares
2 cans (15 ounces each) tomato sauce or 4 cups Tomato Sauce (page 77)
4 medium ripe tomatoes, peeled, seeded, and diced (optional)
1 pound macaroni, cooked according to directions on package
1 cup freshly grated kefalotyri cheese, or more to taste

1. Heat stock to boiling. Add meat and tomato sauce. Simmer until meat is tender (about 2 hours).
2. Add tomato pieces. Simmer 20 minutes. Add cooked macaroni. Heat thoroughly.
3. Top with grated cheese before serving.

8 servings

Fish Soup (Psarosoupa)

2 small cleaned fish or 2 heads and bones from large fish such as red snapper or mackerel (tied together in cheesecloth)
1 bay leaf
2 quarts water or enough to cover
8 or 10 small onions, peeled and left whole
8 or 10 small new potatoes, pared and left whole
3 or 4 carrots, pared and sliced in 1-inch pieces
1 stalk celery, sliced in 1-inch pieces
3 tomatoes, peeled, seeded, and chopped
2 garlic cloves, crushed in a garlic press
2 pounds mackerel fillets
1 pound red snapper fillets
1 pound codfish fillets
Parsley sprigs
Juice of 1 large lemon
½ cup olive oil

1. Put fish heads and bones into a stock pot with bay leaf and water. Bring to a boil and cook 20 minutes, removing scum as it forms. Strain broth; return to pot. Discard heads and bones. Add onions, potatoes, carrots, celery, tomatoes, and garlic. Place mackerel and snapper on top of vegetables. Add water if necessary to cover. Bring to a boil quickly. Boil 10 minutes. Add codfish. Boil another 10 minutes. Remove fish and place in a heated serving dish. Garnish with parsley.
2. Blend lemon juice and olive oil. Drizzle half over fish and add the rest to the stock. Pour soup and vegetables into a tureen. Serve the fish and soup in separate dishes.

8 servings

Tripe Soup

4 pounds prepared tripe
1½ quarts water
Salt and pepper to taste
5 tablespoons butter
2½ tablespoons flour
3 eggs
Juice of 2 lemons
1 teaspoon paprika
Pinch red pepper seeds
Croutons

1. Rinse tripe thoroughly. Place in a large saucepan. Add water, cover, and simmer for 3 hours, adding more water as the water in the pan boils away.
2. Remove tripe from the stock. Put through a meat grinder. Return to the stock. Season with salt and pepper. Cook over medium heat for 2 hours.
3. Meanwhile, melt 3 tablespoons butter in a saucepan, add flour and cook over low heat, stirring constantly, for 3 minutes. Add 1 cup stock in a thick stream to the butter and flour, stirring constantly with a whisk to prevent lumps. Pour this mixture into the soup. Simmer 15 minutes.
4. Beat eggs until frothy. Slowly add lemon juice while beating. Add 2 cups of stock in a thin stream, stirring constantly. Season with paprika and red pepper.
5. Add remaining butter just before serving. Serve with croutons and a cruet of **garlic-flavored vinegar.**

6 to 8 servings

Traditional Greek Easter Soup *(Mayeritsa Avgolemono)*

1 small bunch green onions, trimmed
2 cups diced celery root
4 parsley sprigs
1 dill sprig
2½ quarts water
Salt and freshly ground pepper to taste
½ cup lamb's intestines
½ pound lamb's liver
½ pound lamb's heart
Cold water
½ cup finely chopped parsley
2 tablespoons finely chopped dill
6 egg yolks
Juice of 1 lemon

1. Tie green onions, celery root, parsley, and dill in cheesecloth and place in a kettle. Add the 2½ quarts water, salt, and pepper; bring to a boil.

2. Meanwhile, clean lamb's intestines. Rinse them well, then turn them inside out. To do this, use a small stick about the size of a pencil. Tie one end of one length of intestine. Fit this onto the tip of the stick, then reverse the intestine down the stick much as you would a stocking, pushing the inside out with the fingers. Rinse well and add the intestines to the kettle. Bring to a boil and cook about 1 hour.

3. Place liver and heart in a saucepan and add cold water to cover. Add salt and pepper and simmer until tender (20 minutes or longer).

4. Remove the intestines from the stock. Discard the cheesecloth bag. Chop the intestines. Dice the heart and liver. Add all this to the stock, then add parsley and dill. Heat thoroughly. Strain, reserving stock.

5. Heat small bowl of an electric mixer. Add egg yolks to the bowl and beat well. Add lemon juice, a little at a time, beating rapidly. Beat in 2 cups strained hot stock, tablespoon by tablespoon, beating rapidly. Beat in the remaining stock, strained, and serve immediately.

8 to 10 servings

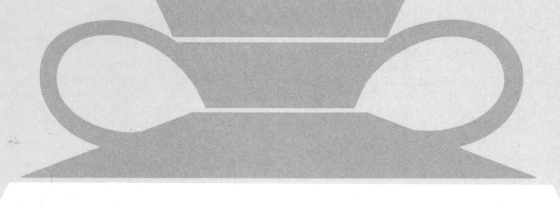

EGGS, YOGURT, AND CHEESE

Frequently, eggs are cooked with other foods as in Moussaka, Kotopita, and Eggs Calomiris. The simpler egg dishes are, for the most part, reserved for children.

Yogurt is considered to be one of the most beneficial foods and is an essential part of the Greek diet. Many attribute a strong constitution and longevity to it. Usually, yogurt is made at home with goat's milk, strained to remove excess liquid, and eaten plain or with honey. In some cities, vendors walk along the streets with pails of yogurt slung across their shoulders calling out "Yaourti" to attract the attention of housewives, who take out bowls to be filled for a few drachmas only.

Feta, kefalotyri, and mizithra are the most popular cheeses. Cheese dishes are ideal for hors d'oeuvres and main courses. Cheese wedges are served at all meals. A simple cheese to make is Yogurt Cheese (page 27).

Fried Eggs with Cheese *(Avga Tyganita me Kefalotyri)*

2 tablespoons olive oil
2 eggs
3 thin slices kefalotyri cheese
Pepper to taste

Heat oil in a skillet until just smoking. Turn heat to very low. Add eggs, then cheese. Cover until whites of eggs are set. Season with pepper.

1 serving

Eggs Calomiris *(Avga Kalomyry)*

3 tablespoons olive oil
1 onion, minced
1 green pepper, minced
1 garlic clove, crushed in a garlic press
1 can (15 ounces) tomato sauce or 2 cups Tomato Sauce (page 77)
2 medium zucchini, scraped and thinly sliced
2 tablespoons minced fresh parsley
1 teaspoon oregano
½ teaspoon thyme
8 eggs
1 cup coarsely grated hard mizithra cheese
Salt and pepper

1. Heat olive oil in a large skillet. Add onion, green pepper, and garlic. Cook until onion is translucent. Add tomato sauce, zucchini, parsley, oregano, and thyme. Cover. Simmer 10 minutes.
2. Slip eggs into the sauce. Top with the cheese. Season with salt and pepper. Cover. Simmer until egg whites are set.

4 servings

Fried Potatoes and Scrambled Eggs *(Patates me Avga Tyganita)*

1 medium potato for each
   serving
Oil for frying
Butter for frying
2 eggs, scrambled, for each
   serving
Salt and pepper to taste

1. Pare potatoes and cut lengthwise into thin strips. Pat dry.
2. Heat oil in a skillet until smoking. Fry potatoes until golden brown. Place on a platter lined with absorbent towels. Keep warm in oven until all potatoes have been fried.
3. Drain oil from skillet and wipe clean. Add butter and melt over low heat.
4. Add potatoes and pour eggs over them. Cook over low heat until eggs are cooked to taste. Season with salt and pepper. Serve immediately.

Shirred Eggs with Feta

1 tablespoon butter
2 eggs
¼ cup crumbled feta cheese
Dash pepper

1. Melt butter in a ramekin or baking dish. Add eggs. Sprinkle with cheese. Season with pepper.
2. Bake at 350°F about 10 minutes, or until eggs are as done as desired.

1 serving

Yogurt *(Yaourti)*

2 to 3 tablespoons prepared
   yogurt
1 quart skimmed or whole milk
½ cup instant nonfat dry milk

1. Allow yogurt to reach room temperature.
2. Bring milk to scalding, then cool to 110° to 115°F. Add dry milk and mix.
3. Dilute yogurt with ½ cup of the milk; mix with the milk. Pour into a bowl.
4. Cover. Wrap with large towel. Set in a warm place 6 to 8 hours (an oven with a pilot light is a good place). When semisolid, store in refrigerator.

About 1 quart

Note: Serve with honey as a dessert or plain as an accompaniment to Rice with Pine Nuts (page 78).

Yogurt Cheese

2 quarts Yogurt
Salt to taste
Honey (optional)

1. Pour Yogurt into a bag made of several thicknesses of cheesecloth. Suspend bag from a nail or sink faucet and drain several hours or overnight.
2. Remove cheese from bag. Chill.
3. To serve, sprinkle lightly with salt and spread on bread. Spoon honey over top.

Scrambled Eggs with Tomato *(Avga me Domata)*

1 large ripe tomato
3 tablespoons butter or olive oil
2 eggs
 Salt

1. To peel tomato, bring 2 cups of water to a boil; turn off the heat. Spear tomato with a fork and plunge it into the water for 1 to 2 minutes, until the skin peels readily. Discard the skin. Cut the tomato into small pieces.

2. In a small skillet, melt 1 tablespoon butter or heat 1 tablespoon of the oil. Add the tomato pieces, stirring constantly until all the liquid has evaporated. Set the tomato aside.

3. Break eggs into a bowl; beat slightly. Melt remaining butter or heat the oil in a skillet. Pour in the eggs and add the tomato. Stir constantly until eggs are set. Serve at once. Season with salt.

1 serving

BREADS

The staple bread of Greece is shaped into a large round loaf with a thick, crisp crust and a feather-light interior. Village bread, on the other hand, is much heavier. Made of whole wheat, it has a flavor and texture which is difficult to reproduce in America because of the difference in the kinds of wheat available. Traditionally, bread is made at home and then taken to a communal oven for baking.

Bread is a vital ingredient at any meal and it plays an important part in Greek culture. During church services, a special bread, Prosphoron, becomes the Body of Christ (see page 92). Thus, all bread is treated with reverence. Because of its religious connotations, when a piece falls to the floor, Greeks pick it up and kiss it.

Rich breads are baked for special occasions and holidays. Sometimes a cook will rely on one recipe but vary it for the occasion. Easter Bread, Lambropsomo, is decorated with red eggs. At New Year's, the bread is made into Vasilopita by dropping a coin into the dough before baking.

Greek Easter Bread *(Lambropsomo)*

2 packages active dry yeast
½ cup warm water
½ cup milk, scalded and cooled
1 cup unsalted butter, melted and cooled to lukewarm
4 eggs, slightly beaten
1 egg yolk
¾ cup sugar
1 tablespoon anise seed, crushed
1 teaspoon salt
7 cups all-purpose flour
1 egg white, slightly beaten
¼ cup sesame seed

1. Blend yeast with warm water in a large bowl and stir until dissolved. Add milk, butter, eggs, egg yolk, sugar, anise seed, and salt; blend thoroughly. Add flour gradually, beating until smooth.
2. Turn dough onto a lightly floured board and knead for 10 minutes, or until dough is smooth and elastic.
3. Place dough in a lightly oiled large bowl, turning dough to coat surface. Cover and let rise in a warm place for about 2 hours, or until double in bulk. Test by inserting a finger about ½ inch into dough. If indentation remains, the dough is ready to shape.
4. Punch dough down. Knead on unfloured board to make a smooth ball. Cut off four pieces, each the size of a large egg. Place remaining dough in a greased round pan, 10 inches in diameter and 2 inches high. Shape small pieces into twists about 4½ inches long. Arrange the twists from the center of the dough so they radiate out to the edge. Brush the loaf lightly with beaten egg white. Sprinkle with sesame seed. Cover loaf lightly and set in a warm place until double in bulk (about 1½ hours).
5. Bake at 375°F for 30 minutes, or until a wooden pick inserted in center of loaf comes out clean. Transfer to wire rack to cool.

1 large loaf

Note: For Easter, place a red egg in center of the dough in pan. Shape small pieces of dough into loops and place a red egg in the center of each.

New Year's Day Bread (Vasilopita): Follow recipe for Greek Easter Bread; substitute **grated peel of 1 large orange** for the anise seed. Wrap a coin in foil and knead into the dough. Proceed as directed.

Christmas Bread *(Christopsomo)*

2 envelopes active dry yeast
2 cups scalded milk, cooled to 105° to 115°F
1 cup sugar
1 teaspoon salt
4 eggs (or 8 yolks), well beaten
½ cup unsalted butter, melted
7½ to 8 cups all-purpose flour
1½ teaspoons cardamom, pounded, or 1 teaspoon mastic
½ cup dried golden currants
¾ cup chopped walnuts
2 egg whites, beaten
3 to 4 tablespoons sugar

1. Sprinkle yeast over 1 cup warm milk in a small bowl; stir until dissolved. Set aside.
2. Reserve 2 teaspoons sugar for pounding with mastic, if using. Put sugar into a bowl and add salt, eggs, remaining 1 cup milk, and butter; mix well.
3. Put 7 cups flour into a large bowl. Stir in cardamom, or pound mastic with 2 teaspoons sugar (so it will not become gummy) and add. Make a well and add dissolved yeast, egg mixture, currants, and nuts; mix well.
4. Knead dough on a floured board, adding the remaining 1 cup flour as required. Knead dough until smooth (5 to 6 minutes).
5. Place dough in a greased bowl. Turn until surface is completely greased. Cover. Set in a warm place until double in bulk.
6. Punch dough down. Form into two round loaves and place in buttered 10-inch pans.
7. Cover and let rise again in a warm place until double in bulk.
8. Bake at 375°F 15 minutes. Remove from oven and brush with beaten egg whites, then sprinkle with sugar. Return to oven. Turn oven control to 325°F and bake about 35 to 40 minutes, or until bread is done.

2 loaves

Island Bread

2 packages active dry yeast
1½ cups warm water (105° to 115°F)
¼ cup packed dark brown sugar
2 tablespoons honey
3 cups whole wheat flour
¼ cup olive oil
2 tablespoons grated orange peel
1 tablespoon grated lemon peel
2½ teaspoons salt
1 teaspoon anise seed, crushed
2 cups all-purpose flour

1. Dissolve yeast in warm water; stir in brown sugar, honey, and whole wheat flour. Beat with a wooden spoon until smooth. Cover and let rise in a warm place until almost double in bulk (about 2 hours).
2. Stir in oil, orange and lemon peels, salt, and anise seed. Gradually add 1¾ cups all-purpose flour, beating vigorously. Cover for 10 minutes.
3. Sprinkle remaining ¼ cup flour on a board and work it in. Put dough on board, cover, and let rise until double in bulk. Shape into a round loaf; put onto a well-greased cookie sheet.
4. Let rise until dough is double in bulk.
5. Bake at 375°F 45 minutes. Turn out of pan immediately and cool on a rack.

1 loaf

Sourdough Greek Bread

5 to 5½ cups all-purpose flour
2 cups warm water (105° to 115°F)
½ cup Starter
3 tablespoons sugar
1 package active dry yeast
2 teaspoons salt
1½ teaspoons baking soda

1. Combine 2 cups flour, water, Starter, and sugar in a large glass bowl, beating until smooth. Cover with waxed paper and let stand in a warm place (80° to 85°F) at least 36 hours, stirring batter down every day.
2. Combine yeast, salt, baking soda, and 1 cup flour. Add to starter mixture and stir until well blended. Stir in the remaining flour, using enough to make a moderately stiff dough. Turn onto lightly floured surface and knead until smooth and satiny (10 to 15 minutes).
3. Put into a large deep bowl and cover with plastic wrap or aluminum foil. Let rise in a warm place until double in bulk (about 2 hours).
4. Divide dough in half, shape into balls, and place in 2 greased 2-quart round baking dishes. Make a crisscross with a sharp knife on the top of each ball of dough. Cover and let rise in a warm place until double in bulk.
5. Brush loaves with water and place a shallow pan of boiling water on bottom rack of the oven.
6. Bake at 400°F 45 minutes, or until loaves test done. Brush loaves with water twice during baking. Remove from baking dishes immediately; cool.

2 round loaves

Starter

1 package active dry yeast
2 cups warm water
2 cups all-purpose flour

1. Combine yeast, water, and flour in a large glass bowl, mixing until well blended. Let stand uncovered in a warm place for 48 hours, stirring occasionally. Stir well before use.
2. Measure out required amount and replenish remaining starter by mixing in equal parts of flour and water. If ½ cup starter is removed, mix in ¼ cup water and ¼ cup flour to replace. Let starter stand until it bubbles again before covering loosely and refrigerating. Use and replenish every two weeks.

Corn Bread (Bobota)

2 eggs
2 cups buttermilk
3 tablespoons shortening, melted
1½ teaspoons salt
2½ cups cornmeal
1 teaspoon baking powder
½ teaspoon baking soda

1. Beat eggs until light. Add buttermilk and melted shortening; mix well.
2. Mix dry ingredients together. Add to egg mixture; beat until smooth. Pour into a greased 9-inch square baking pan.
3. Bake at 425°F about 25 minutes. Serve hot.

About 16 pieces

Island Bread, 31;
Yogurt Cheese, 27;
Yogurt, 27;
Drop Doughnuts, 34

Whole Wheat Bread

¼ cup warm water (105°F for dry yeast, 95°F for compressed yeast)
1 package yeast, active dry or compressed
1½ cups scalded milk, cooled to 105° or 95°F
½ cup honey
2 tablespoons olive oil
2 tablespoons salt
6 to 6½ cups whole wheat flour

1. Pour water into a bowl; add yeast and stir until dissolved. Add milk, honey, olive oil, and salt. Stir with a wooden spoon until well blended.
2. Stir in 4 cups of flour, 1 cup at a time. Beat until dough is smooth and elastic. Mix in another cup of flour. The dough will be very stiff.
3. Measure another cup of flour; sprinkle half of it on a board. Turn dough onto the board. Knead dough, adding flour to board until the dough no longer sticks. Continue kneading until dough is not sticky (about 8 minutes).
4. Put dough into a greased bowl about three times the size of the dough. Turn dough to grease surface lightly. Cover bowl with a towel and let rise in a warm place for about 2 hours, or until double in bulk. Test by inserting a finger about ½ inch into dough. If indentation remains, the dough is ready to shape.
5. Punch dough down; squeeze out air bubbles and shape into a smooth ball. Let rise again in warm place for about 30 minutes.
6. Divide into equal portions for 2 loaves. Form each into a smooth oval loaf. Let stand covered for 15 minutes.
7. Place the loaves seam side down in 2 greased 9x5x3-inch loaf pans. Cover with a towel and let rise in warm place until almost double in bulk (about 1 hour).
8. Bake at 375°F about 30 minutes, or until crust is medium brown.
9. Turn out of pans at once. Cool on wire racks.

2 loaves

Oregano and Kefalotyri Cheese Bread
(Psomi me Rigani ke Kefalotyri)

3 to 3½ cups all-purpose flour
2 tablespoons sugar
1½ teaspoons salt
2 packages active dry yeast
¾ cup milk
¼ cup water
¼ cup shortening
1 egg
3 tablespoons oregano
¼ teaspoon garlic powder
½ cup grated kefalotyri cheese
1 teaspoon mint
2 tablespoons basil
¼ cup instant minced onion
1 tablespoon sesame seed

1. Combine 1 cup flour, sugar, salt, and dry yeast in a large bowl.
2. Heat milk, water, and shortening in a saucepan until warm. (Shortening will not melt completely.) Add milk mixture and egg to flour mixture. Beat until smooth.
3. Mix oregano, garlic powder, cheese, mint, basil, onion, and sesame seed. Stir into dough. Gradually add more flour to form a stiff dough.
4. Turn into a greased loaf pan. Cover with a towel. Let rise in a warm place until double in bulk (about 1 hour).
5. Bake at 350°F about 40 minutes, or until golden brown.

1 loaf

Boiled Endive with Lemon Juice and Olive Oil, 40;
Beans Plaki, 36;
Stuffed Tomatoes with Rice and Pine Nuts, 42

Drop Doughnuts (Svingi)

4 eggs
1 cup buttermilk
2 teaspoons vanilla extract
1 teaspoon grated lemon or
     orange peel (optional)
3 cups all-purpose flour
1½ teaspoons baking powder
     Cooking oil for deep frying
     Honey
     Cinnamon

1. Beat eggs; stir in buttermilk, vanilla extract, and grated peel. Combine flour and baking powder. Stir into the egg mixture. Cover with a cloth. Let stand at room temperature for 1 hour.
2. In a deep fryer, heat oil to 375°F. Drop batter by the tablespoon. Cook 4 minutes, or until doughnuts are golden brown. Drain on paper towels. Drizzle with honey and sprinkle with cinnamon. Serve hot.

About 30 doughnuts

Note: Batter keeps well in the refrigerator. Bring to room temperature before cooking.

VEGETABLES

Greeks prefer fresh vegetables which vary, of course, according to season. Vegetable dishes are served hot or at room temperature, rarely chilled. They may be served as main courses, especially during periods of fasting, and as salads, as side dishes, or as hors d'oeuvres.

In the spring, both in Greece and America, one often sees people in parks and on roadways pulling up tender new endives for an evening's meal. These "antithia" may be served simply with olive oil and lemon juice, or as a hearty dish with meat and an egg and lemon sauce.

While the Greek cuisine has many rich vegetable dishes, a favorite cooking method among gourmets, particularly those who watch their weight, is simply to simmer vegetables in water or stock until just tender and then to season them with lemon juice and olive oil.

Artichokes in White Wine *(Angynares Krasata)*

12 whole small onions, peeled
 1 cup wine
 1 cup water
 ¾ cup olive oil
   Salt and pepper to taste
 1 teaspoon sugar
 1 teaspoon marjoram
 1 bay leaf
 4 parsley sprigs, minced
   Juice of 1 lemon
 8 artichokes, cleaned and cut in
   quarters

1. Combine all ingredients in a deep saucepan. Simmer covered until artichokes are tender.
2. Serve either hot or cold.

4 servings

Beans Plaki

 3 cups dried white beans
 ½ cup olive oil
 2 medium onions, chopped
 2 garlic cloves, crushed in a
   garlic press
 1 can (8 ounces) tomato sauce or
   1 cup Tomato Sauce (page
   77)
 2 celery stalks, diced
 1 carrot, diced
 1 bay leaf
 1 teaspoon oregano
 1 teaspoon sugar
   Salt and pepper to taste
   Wine vinegar

1. Place beans in a pot and cover with water. Bring to a boil. Simmer covered 2 to 3 hours, until just tender. Drain.
2. Heat oil in a saucepan, add onion, and cook until translucent. Add garlic, tomato sauce, celery, carrot, bay leaf, oregano, sugar, salt, and pepper. Simmer 5 minutes. (If sauce is too thick, add a little water.)
3. Add beans to sauce and simmer covered about 20 minutes, or until tender.
4. Serve hot or cold with a cruet of wine vinegar.

About 12 servings

Green Beans with Tomatoes *(Fasolakia me Domates)*

2 pounds green beans or 3
    packages (9 ounces each)
    frozen green beans
1 teaspoon salt
½ cup olive oil
1 can (20 ounces) tomatoes
    (undrained)
1 medium onion, chopped
    Juice of 1 lemon
1 teaspoon oregano, crushed
    Salt and pepper

1. Wash green beans, cut off ends, and cut in half lengthwise. Bring a small amount of water to a boil. Add ½ teaspoon salt and the beans. Cover and cook about 20 minutes. Drain. If frozen beans are used, cook according to directions on the package.
2. Heat olive oil in a skillet. Add tomatoes, onion, lemon juice, oregano, and salt and pepper to taste. Simmer covered 10 minutes. Pour over beans. Simmer together an additional 10 minutes.

8 servings

Green Beans with Onion Rings

1 cup water
1 onion, thinly sliced
2 pounds green beans, ends
    snipped off and beans sliced
½ cup butter
    Salt and pepper to taste
    Lemon juice to taste

Bring water to boiling. Separate onion slices into rings and add. Add green beans, butter, salt, pepper, and lemon juice. Boil until beans are tender (about 20 minutes).

6 servings

Stewed Cabbage in Tomato Sauce *(Lahana Brasto me Domata)*

1 head cabbage
    Boiling salted water
½ cup olive oil
1 medium onion, chopped
1 can (16 ounces) tomatoes
    (undrained)
1 celery stalk, diced
1 carrot, diced
1 bay leaf
1 teaspoon sugar
    Salt and pepper to taste

1. Remove outer leaves from cabbage and trim off part of the core. Drop into boiling salted water to cover. Cook until just tender (about 8 minutes). Drain.
2. Meanwhile, heat olive oil in a saucepan and add onion; cook until translucent. Add tomatoes, celery, carrot, bay leaf, and sugar. Simmer 15 minutes.
3. Pour sauce over cabbage. Season with salt and pepper.

4 servings

Baked Carrot Ring

¾ cup butter
2 eggs, separated
½ cup packed brown sugar
1 teaspoon cinnamon
½ teaspoon nutmeg
½ teaspoon mint
    Juice of ½ lemon
2 teaspoons water
1½ cups grated carrots
1 cup dried black currants
1 cup pine nuts
1 cup all-purpose flour
1 teaspoon baking powder
½ teaspoon baking soda
½ teaspoon salt
½ cup cracker meal

1. Using an electric mixer, cream butter, egg yolks, brown sugar, cinnamon, nutmeg, and mint until fluffy. Add lemon juice, water, carrots, currants, and pine nuts; blend thoroughly.
2. Mix flour, baking powder, baking soda, and salt. Add to carrot mixture.
3. Beat egg whites until fluffy. Fold into batter.
4. Grease a 9-inch ring mold or a square cake pan. Sprinkle with cracker meal. Pour in the batter.
5. Bake at 350°F 50 to 55 minutes.
6. Cool on wire rack. Place a serving dish over the top of carrot ring. Invert to unmold.

8 servings

Dilled Carrots *(Karota me Anitho)*

1 cup water
¼ cup white wine vinegar
1 medium onion, quartered
½ teaspoon salt
1 tablespoon dill
6 large carrots, pared and cut in thick slices

1. Bring water and vinegar to boiling. Put in onion, salt, dill, and carrots. Reduce heat and simmer 10 minutes. Cool.
2. Refrigerate in liquid until chilled.
3. Drain and serve cold.

4 to 6 servings

Cauliflower in Béchamel Sauce *(Kounoupidi me Béchamel Saltsa)*

1 head cauliflower
    Boiling water
    Juice of 1 small lemon
2 cups Béchamel Sauce (page 65)
½ cup grated mizithra cheese
¼ cup fresh bread crumbs
¼ teaspoon ground allspice
    Salt and pepper to taste

1. Remove leaves from the cauliflower and cut off tough end. Soak in cold salted water for 15 minutes. Rinse and drain. Keep whole or break into flowerets.
2. Boil enough water to cover cauliflower. Add lemon juice and the cauliflower. Cook until stalks are just tender (10 to 20 minutes). Drain.
3. Place cauliflower in a baking dish. Cover with Béchamel Sauce, sprinkle with cheese, bread crumbs, allspice, salt, and pepper.
4. Bake at 375°F 20 minutes.

4 to 6 servings

Stewed Cauliflower (Kounoupidi Sigovrasmeno)

1 head cauliflower
½ cup olive oil
1 medium onion, chopped
1 garlic clove
1 bay leaf
1 tablespoon wine vinegar
¼ cup chopped parsley

1. Remove leaves from cauliflower and cut off tough end. Soak in cold salted water for 15 minutes. Rinse and drain. Keep whole or break into flowerets.
2. Heat olive oil in a saucepan. Add onion and cook until translucent. Add garlic, bay leaf, wine vinegar, parsley, cauliflower, and enough water to cover. Cover. Simmer, turning several times until tender (10 to 20 minutes).
3. Serve hot or cooled.

4 servings

Fried Eggplant (Melitzanes Tyganites)

2 medium eggplants
Salt
¾ cup olive oil
¾ cup vegetable oil
2 cups all-purpose flour
Salt and pepper to taste

1. Slice eggplants horizontally 1/3 inch thick. Sprinkle both sides generously with salt. Arrange in a single layer in baking dish. Allow to stand 1 hour.
2. Squeeze each eggplant slice firmly between palms of hands or use a heavy weight wrapped in aluminum foil to press out excess liquid.
3. Heat oils together to smoking.
4. Meanwhile, season flour with salt and pepper. Dip each slice in the flour. Fry the eggplant slices until golden brown, turning once. Remove. Serve immediately.

About 6 servings

Stuffed Eggplant (Melitzanes Yemistes)

¼ cup olive oil
2 large onions, minced
1 cup minced celery
1 carrot, thinly sliced
1 tablespoon long-grain rice
1 garlic clove, crushed in a garlic press
⅓ cup chopped parsley
1 teaspoon mint
½ teaspoon oregano
½ teaspoon thyme
1 can (8 ounces) whole tomatoes, drained
Salt and pepper to taste
1 firm ripe eggplant

1. Heat oil in a large skillet, add onion, and sauté. Remove from heat. Add celery, carrot, rice, garlic, parsley, mint, oregano, thyme, tomatoes, salt, and pepper. Cover. Simmer 10 to 15 minutes.
2. Cut off the stem end of the eggplant. Scoop out the center pulp. Sprinkle inside with salt. Set shell aside. Mash pulp and add to vegetables. Simmer, stirring occasionally, for 10 minutes.
3. Rinse inside of eggplant with a little water. Spoon in vegetable mixture. Replace top and secure with wooden picks.
4. Pour ½ cup water into a baking pan. Place eggplant on a trivet in pan.
5. Bake at 350°F 1 hour.
6. To serve, slice eggplant in half from top to bottom. Lay portions flat. Slice each lengthwise again.

4 servings

Boiled Endive with Lemon Juice and Olive Oil
(Vrasta Antithia)

2 bunches young curly endive
3 cups water
1 teaspoon salt
1 lemon, cut in wedges, or use
    wine vinegar
  Olive oil

1. Slice endive in half lengthwise. Rinse several times to remove all traces of dirt. Cut stem 1 inch from bottom and discard.
2. Boil the endive in water with salt added in a covered pot until tender (about 20 to 25 minutes).
3. Serve with lemon juice and olive oil.

4 servings

Braised Leeks (Prassa Vrasta)

¼ cup lemon juice
6 tablespoons olive oil
1½ cups chicken stock
1 teaspoon fennel seed, crushed
1 teaspoon coriander seed,
    crushed
½ teaspoon thyme
1 bay leaf
1 garlic clove, sliced
  Salt and pepper to taste
9 medium leeks, white part only,
    split and cleaned, attached at
    the root

1. Combine lemon juice, olive oil, chicken stock, fennel seed, coriander seed, thyme, bay leaf, garlic, salt, and pepper in a skillet and bring to boiling. Simmer covered 15 minutes.
2. Arrange the prepared leeks in skillet in one layer. Simmer covered 20 to 30 minutes, or until tender.
3. Remove leeks carefully, arrange on serving platter, and pour liquid over.

3 servings

Okra with Tomatoes (Bamies Giahni me Lathi)

2 pounds fresh okra
½ cup olive oil
1 large onion, minced
5 tomatoes, peeled, seeded, and
    coarsely chopped
3 garlic cloves, halved
1 teaspoon sugar
  Salt and pepper to taste
  Juice of 1 lemon

1. Wash okra and cut off any hard stems. Blanch in salted water for 3 minutes.
2. Heat olive oil. Add onion and cook until translucent. Add okra and cook until it begins to soften. Add tomatoes, garlic, sugar, salt, and pepper. Cook 2 to 3 minutes. Pour in enough water to cover. Cover and simmer about 1 hour, or until okra is tender. Stir in lemon juice. Serve hot.

8 servings

Simmered Zucchini

6 zucchini (5 inches long), cut in
    thick slices
1 cup water
½ cup olive oil
¼ cup wine vinegar
1 parsley sprig
1 garlic clove
  Salt and pepper to taste

Combine all ingredients in a saucepan. Bring to a boil and reduce heat. Simmer covered about 8 minutes, or until just tender. Let cool in the liquid. Serve hot or chilled.

6 servings

Potato Cakes *(Patates Keftethes)*

2 pounds potatoes
3 tablespoons grated kefalotyri cheese
2 tablespoons chopped parsley
Salt and pepper to taste
6 eggs, beaten
1 garlic clove, crushed in a garlic press
Flour for coating
Oil for frying

1. Boil potatoes in skins until tender. Peel and mash thoroughly. Mix in cheese, parsley, salt, pepper, eggs, and garlic. Shape into flat cakes. Coat with flour.
2. Heat oil in a skillet and add cakes, a few at a time. Fry until golden brown, turning once.

6 servings

Spinach Casserole

4 packages (10 ounces each) frozen spinach, defrosted
7 slices day-old whole wheat bread with crusts removed
Water
¼ cup olive oil
3 garlic cloves, crushed in a garlic press
2 bunches scallions, minced
1 leek, minced
½ pound mushrooms
Salt and pepper to taste
2 tablespoons dill weed
1 tablespoon oregano
½ teaspoon cinnamon
1 tablespoon mint
6 eggs, beaten
¾ cup grated kefalotyri cheese
1½ cups water or chicken broth
1 cup freshly toasted coarse bread crumbs
Olive oil

1. Squeeze excess liquid from spinach. Sprinkle bread slices with water. Squeeze water out.
2. Heat olive oil in a large skillet. Sauté garlic, scallions, leek, and mushrooms for 3 minutes. Remove from heat. Add salt, pepper, dill, oregano, cinnamon, mint, and spinach. Sauté the mixture for 3 minutes. Add bread, eggs, cheese, and water; mix well.
3. Oil a 3½-quart baking dish and sprinkle bottom with bread crumbs. Pour in the spinach mixture.
4. Bake at 350°F 40 to 50 minutes, or until mixture is firm.

8 to 12 servings

Spinach with Rice *(Spanakorizo)*

1 medium onion, finely chopped
3 tablespoons olive oil
1 pound fresh spinach, washed well and drained, or 2 packages (10 ounces each) frozen leaf spinach, partially thawed
1 tablespoon tomato paste
¼ cup water
2 tablespoons long-grain rice
Salt and pepper to taste

In a saucepan, cook onion in olive oil until translucent. Add the spinach. Mix tomato paste with the water and add along with rice; cover. Simmer until rice is tender (about 20 minutes). Season with salt and pepper.

4 servings

Stuffed Tomatoes with Rice and Pine Nuts
(Domates Yemistes Neptisima)

8 large firm tomatoes with tops sliced off and reserved
Salt, pepper, and sugar to taste
¾ cup olive oil
4 onions, minced
1 cup long-grain rice
½ cup water
½ cup chopped parsley
½ cup dried currants
½ cup pine nuts
1 teaspoon mint
Juice of 1 lemon
2 cups water

1. Scoop out pulp from tomatoes and reserve. Sprinkle insides of tomatoes with salt, pepper, and sugar. Arrange in a baking dish.
2. Heat ¼ cup oil in a large skillet. Add onion, pulp, rice, water, parsley, currants, pine nuts, mint, and lemon juice. Simmer, covered, stirring occasionally, until liquid is absorbed. Cool slightly. Adjust seasonings.
3. Fill tomatoes with rice mixture. Replace tops and put into baking dish. Drizzle remaining olive oil between tomatoes. Add water.
4. Bake at 350°F about 40 minutes, or until rice is cooked; baste occasionally. If necessary, add a little water. Serve hot or chilled.

6 servings

Grilled Tomatoes with Rosemary and Dill

6 large ripe red tomatoes, cored and sliced in half horizontally
¼ cup olive oil
3 teaspoons rosemary
2 teaspoons dill
12 teaspoons grated kefalotyri cheese
Salt and pepper to taste

1. Arrange tomatoes, cut side up, in a baking dish. Pour olive oil onto tomatoes, letting some fall into the dish.
2. Sprinkle with rosemary, dill, and cheese. Season with salt and pepper.
3. Broil until topping begins to brown (about 5 minutes).

6 servings

Steamed Yellow Squash *(Kolokithia Vrasta)*

1 can (10 ounces) plum tomatoes
1 large onion, minced
1 tablespoon minced parsley
1 teaspoon mint
1 teaspoon oregano
Salt and pepper to taste
1 cup chicken stock
3 tablespoons butter
2 pounds small yellow squash, sliced in half lengthwise

Combine all ingredients except squash. Bring to a boil. Add squash. Reduce heat and simmer about 15 minutes, or until squash is tender.

6 servings

Mixed Baked Vegetables *(Tourlou Tava)*

1 pound fresh green beans, ends snipped off and beans sliced vertically
2 large potatoes, pared and quartered
2 medium zucchini, pared and cut in ½-inch slices
4 celery stalks, cut in ½-inch slices
1 can (20 ounces) whole tomatoes, quartered, or 4 fresh tomatoes, peeled and cut in wedges
2 large onions, peeled and sliced
3 tablespoons olive oil
2 garlic cloves, crushed in a garlic press
½ cup chopped parsley
½ cup chopped dill
Salt and pepper to taste
Warm water

1. Oil a 2½-quart casserole. Arrange green beans, potatoes, zucchini, celery, tomatoes, and onions in layers, drizzling with oil and seasoning layers with garlic, parsley, dill, salt, and pepper. Add enough water to reach three fourths the depth of vegetables. Cover casserole.
2. Bake at 400°F about 15 minutes, or until liquid begins to simmer. Turn oven control to 325°F and bake 20 minutes longer. Remove cover and bake another 10 minutes. Adjust seasoning.

6 servings

Cooked Vegetables with Garlic Mayonnaise

1 cup french-cut green beans, cooked
1 cup green peas, cooked
4 artichoke hearts, cooked
1 cup broccoli pieces, cooked
1 cup cauliflowerets, cooked
Paprika
Garlic Mayonnaise
Parsley sprigs for garnish

Arrange vegetables in separate mounds in a serving dish, leaving a space in the center. Sprinkle with paprika. Mound Garlic Mayonnaise in the center. Garnish with parsley.

6 to 8 servings

Garlic Mayonnaise *(Mayoneza me Skortho)*

4 garlic cloves, crushed in a garlic press
¼ teaspoon salt
2 egg yolks
Olive oil (about 1 cup)
Juice of ½ lemon, or more to taste
Salt and white pepper

Combine garlic, salt, and egg yolks. Slowly add oil, a drop at a time, beating vigorously until 2 to 3 tablespoons have been added. Add remaining oil in a steady stream, beating constantly. Add lemon juice, beating well. Season with salt and pepper.

About 1½ cups

Cucumber Salad *(Tsatziki)*

2 cups plain yogurt
1 scallion, chopped
1 teaspoon mint
½ teaspoon salt
  Freshly ground pepper
  Pinch dill
1 garlic clove, crushed in a garlic press
4 cucumbers, pared and thinly sliced

Mix yogurt with scallion, mint, salt, pepper, dill, and garlic. Add cucumber and toss to coat with dressing. Refrigerate 1 hour.

6 servings

Potato Salad *(Patatosalata)*

½ cup olive oil
3 tablespoons wine vinegar
1 teaspoon oregano, crushed
2 tablespoons chopped parsley
1 medium onion, finely sliced
5 large red potatoes
  Salt and pepper to taste

1. Combine olive oil, vinegar, oregano, parsley, and onion. Mix well. Set aside to marinate.
2. Scrub potatoes. Boil them in salted water in their jackets. When just tender (about 40 minutes), remove and plunge into cold water so they can be handled at once. Peel while hot and cut into even slices.
3. Pour the dressing over the potatoes; toss lightly. Add salt and pepper.

6 servings

Anchovy Potato Salad

Dressing:
1 cup olive oil
½ cup wine vinegar
¼ teaspoon sugar
1 teaspoon dill
1 teaspoon marjoram
  Pepper to taste

Salad:
8 Anchovy Fillets (page 18) or 1 can (2 ounces) anchovies preserved in olive oil, drained
1 bunch escarole, torn in bite-size pieces
2 potatoes, boiled and diced
1 small jar pickled beets, drained and diced
2 green peppers, cleaned and thinly sliced
4 scallions, minced
3 hard-cooked eggs, sliced, for garnish
1 teaspoon capers for garnish
  Salt and pepper to taste

1. For dressing, combine all ingredients in a jar. Shake well. Refrigerate 1 or 2 hours before serving.
2. For salad, combine anchovies with remaining ingredients, except eggs, capers, salt, and pepper. Add the salad dressing and toss to coat. Garnish with eggs and capers. Season with salt and pepper.

4 to 6 servings

Cucumber and Tomato Salad *(Angourodomatosalata)*

3 firm-ripe homegrown tomatoes,
   cut in wedges
3 pickle cucumbers (as straight
   as possible), pared and sliced
   ¼ inch thick
4 scallions, finely chopped
¼ pound feta cheese, crumbled
   Kalamata olives (about 8)
   Oregano and freshly dried dill,
   a generous pinch of each
   Salt and pepper to taste
3 tablespoons wine vinegar
⅓ cup olive oil

1. In a salad bowl, combine tomatoes, cucumbers, scallions, cheese, and olives. Season with oregano, dill, salt, and pepper.
2. Combine vinegar and olive oil in a small jar; shake well. Add to salad and toss.

6 to 8 servings

Lobster Salad *(Astakos Mayoneza)*

6 cups diced fresh lobster meat,
   chilled
3 hard-cooked eggs, mashed
   through a sieve
1 large scallion, minced
1 small leek, finely chopped
2 teaspoons tarragon
½ teaspoon thyme
2 garlic cloves, crushed in a
   garlic press
2 cups Mayonnaise
1 tablespoon capers
   Juice of 1 lemon
   Cucumber, sliced paper thin
   Tomato wedges for garnish

1. Combine all ingredients except cucumber and tomato. Adjust seasoning.
2. Spoon into heated **pastry shells,** a **lobster** cavity, or on a bed of **lettuce.** Garnish with cucumber slices and tomato wedges.

About 12 servings

Mayonnaise *(Mayoneza)*

2 egg yolks
½ teaspoon salt
¼ teaspoon white pepper
½ teaspoon dry mustard
   Wine or tarragon vinegar
   (about 3 tablespoons)
1½ cups olive oil

Beat egg yolks until thick and lemon colored. Beat in salt, pepper, dry mustard, and half of the vinegar. Beating constantly, trickle in 1/3 cup olive oil, add ½ teaspoon vinegar, and trickle in remaining olive oil. Check for consistency. If the Mayonnaise is too thick, add vinegar drop by drop and mix by hand until the appropriate consistency is achieved. Adjust seasoning.

About 1½ cups

Note: If Mayonnaise curdles, wash beater. Beat an egg yolk until thick in a small bowl. Slowly add curdled mixture, beating constantly, to form a new emulsion. Another egg yolk may be necessary. If so, beat again until thick, add mixture slowly.

Russian Salad *(Salata Roseiki)*

⅓ cup olive oil
3 tablespoons vinegar
1 cup diced cooked carrots
1 cup diced cooked beets
2 potatoes, cooked and diced
1 cup french-cut green beans,
    cooked and diced
1 cup cooked peas
¼ cup minced parsley
    Mayonnaise (page 45)
    Salt and pepper to taste
2 teaspoons capers

1. Mix olive oil and vinegar and pour over vegetables; allow to marinate 1 to 2 hours. Drain. Discard dressing.
2. Mix vegetables and parsley with enough Mayonnaise to bind together (about 1 cup). Season with salt and pepper. Garnish with capers to serve.

6 servings

Note: Russian Salad makes an excellent appetizer. Serve in small dishes with heated **Sourdough Greek Bread** (page 32).

SEAFOOD

The salt waters of the Mediterranean, Aegean, and Ionian seas that surround the rocky foothills of Greece are the source of delectable seafood without peer anywhere in the world.

Shellfish abound in the Greek seas. Sea urchins are eaten raw within minutes of being brought up by swimmers who have dived into the clear waters to pry them loose from the rocks to which they were fastened.

Greeks eat fish more frequently than meat, and rely on it especially during the periods of fasting when, on special days, they are permitted to break their fast with seafood.

There is no substitute for fresh fish, seasoned simply with lemon juice and oregano and drizzled lightly with olive oil before being broiled.

Baked Halibut in Parchment Paper

1 tablespoon olive oil
Juice of ½ lemon
Pinch basil
Pinch oregano
1 halibut steak (or any other preferred steak)
Salt and pepper
2 thin lemon slices
4 capers

1. Combine oil, lemon juice, basil, and oregano; spoon over both sides of the fish. Season with salt and pepper.
2. Place the fish on a piece of parchment paper. Lay lemon slices and capers on top of fish. Seal paper and tie. Put into a baking dish.
3. Bake at 325°F 30 minutes.
4. Serve hot sealed in parchment.

1 serving

Fried Codfish in Garlic Sauce
(Bakaliaros Tiganitos me Skorthalia)

4 frozen codfish fillets, thawed
Flour, seasoned with salt and pepper
Flour and water to make a thick paste (about 1¼ cups water to 1 cup flour)
Oil for frying
Garlic and Potato Sauce
Lemon wedges

1. Pat fillets dry. Coat with seasoned flour. Dip in flour and water mixture.
2. Pour oil into a deep skillet and heat to smoking.
3. Put fillets in oil. Fry until golden brown, turning once.
4. Serve with Garlic and Potato Sauce and lemon wedges.

2 to 4 servings

Garlic and Potato Sauce (Skorthalia)

1 pound potatoes, pared and cut in small pieces
4 garlic cloves, crushed in a garlic press
1 cup olive oil
¼ cup vinegar
Salt and freshly ground pepper

1. Boil potatoes until they can be pierced easily with a fork. Drain in a colander or on paper towels.
2. Mash potatoes in a potato ricer. Add garlic and then olive oil, a tablespoon at a time, beating well after each spoonful. Beat in vinegar. Season with salt and pepper to taste. If sauce is too thick, beat in a little warm water or more olive oil.
3. Serve with **fried** or **broiled seafood,** on **crackers** or **toasted bread,** or as a dip for **fresh vegetables.**

1 quart sauce

Baked Fish à la Spetses

4 pounds fish fillets (turbot,
    whitefish, bass, mullet)
4 fresh tomatoes, peeled and
    sliced
¾ cup olive oil
1 cup white wine
2 tablespoons chopped parsley
1 large garlic clove, crushed in a
    garlic press
  Salt and pepper to taste
1 teaspoon basil (optional)
1 cup fresh bread crumbs
1 slice feta cheese for each
    portion

1. Put fillets into a baking dish.
2. In a bowl, combine tomatoes, olive oil, wine, parsley, garlic, salt, pepper, and basil. Pour over fillets. Sprinkle with bread crumbs.
3. Bake at 375°F 40 minutes.
4. Top fillets with feta cheese slices. Broil 1 or 2 minutes.

6 to 8 servings

Charcoal-Grilled Fish *(Psari tys Skaras)*

  Fish for grilling
¼ cup olive oil
  Juice of 1 lemon
2 tablespoons oregano, crushed
  Salt and pepper to taste

1. Fish suitable for grilling are trout, whitefish, bluefish, snapper, or mackerel. (In Greece, the fish are usually served with their heads and tails intact. You may prefer to remove the heads at least, because some people are revolted by a whole fish on their plate. However you decide to serve the fish, allow 1 pound for each person.)
2. Heat charcoal until white. Arrange grill so that it is about 4 inches from coals. Use a hinged basket grill for easier turning; oil it well to prevent fish from sticking.
3. Combine olive oil, lemon juice, oregano, salt, and pepper. Brush fish generously with mixture. Place in basket grill.
4. Cook on one side about 7 minutes. Turn over and cook an additional 7 minutes.
5. Serve fish with remaining sauce.

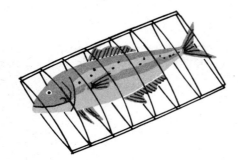

Baked Fish with Tomatoes, Onions, and Parsley *(Psari Plaki)*

½ cup olive oil
2 large onions, coarsely chopped
1 can (20 ounces) tomatoes
    (undrained)
½ cup white wine
½ cup chopped parsley
1 garlic clove, crushed in a garlic
    press
  Salt and pepper to taste
3 pounds fish fillets (any firm
    fish such as turbot, bass,
    grouper, or red snapper may
    be used)

1. Heat olive oil in a saucepan. Add onion and cook until translucent. Add tomatoes, wine, parsley, garlic, salt, and pepper. Simmer covered 10 minutes.
2. Place fish in a large baking dish. Cover with sauce.
3. Bake at 350°F about 25 minutes, or until fish flakes easily when tested with a fork.

4 servings

Fish Kebob

2 pounds swordfish or halibut
  with bones removed, cut in
  large cubes
1 cup olive oil
  Juice of 2 lemons
1 teaspoon oregano
1 teaspoon dill
1 bay leaf
  Salt and pepper to taste
  Small whole onions, peeled
  Whole cherry tomatoes

1. Marinate fish in a mixture of the oil, lemon juice, oregano, dill, bay leaf, salt, and pepper for 2 hours, basting occasionally. Reserve marinade.
2. Alternate fish, onions, and tomatoes on skewers.
3. Broil, turning frequently, until done (about 5 minutes).
4. Heat marinade. Serve with Fish Kebob.

4 servings

Poached Striped Bass

1 quart water
1 quart dry white wine
  Juice of 3 lemons
2 cups olive oil
2 medium onions, quartered
1 large carrot, pared and left
  whole
2 celery stalks with leaves
2 leeks
  Salt to taste
10 coriander seeds
8 whole peppercorns
1 bay leaf
4 parsley sprigs
1 thyme sprig
3 garlic cloves, peeled and left
  whole
5 pounds bass, cleaned, with
  gills removed and head and
  tail left on

1. Pour water, wine, lemon juice, and olive oil into a saucepot.
2. Wrap remaining ingredients, except fish, in cheesecloth and add. Bring to boiling and simmer covered 15 minutes.
3. Wrap fish in cheesecloth. Place in a fish poacher or a deep greased baking dish.
4. Pour in stock, discarding vegetables; cover and simmer 15 minutes. Remove from heat.
5. Let fish remain in the liquid for another 15 minutes. Lift out of pan and drain; reserve fish stock for other use. Remove cheesecloth and peel off skin.
6. Serve fish at room temperature with Vinegar and Oil Dressing with Tomato, Mayonnaise, or Garlic and Potato Sauce (pages 51, 45, 48).

6 to 8 servings

Poached Tuna Rolls with Garlic Mayonnaise

1 can (9¼ ounces) solid-pack
  tuna, drained and flaked
3 anchovies, minced
  ·Salt and pepper to taste
2 eggs, lightly beaten
  Bread crumbs
1 tomato, thinly sliced
1 onion, thinly sliced
1 cucumber, thinly sliced
  Garlic Mayonnaise (page 43)

1. Combine tuna with anchovies. Add pepper and taste before adding salt. Mix in eggs and enough bread crumbs to make a paste firm enough to shape into four 1½-inch-thick rolls.
2. Wrap rolls tightly in cheesecloth. Tie at both ends.
3. Put into boiling salted water to cover. Reduce heat and simmer 20 minutes. Remove from water.
4. Slice rolls and garnish with tomato, onion, and cucumber. Serve with Garlic Mayonnaise.

4 servings

Fish Casserole Haramogli *(Psari Haramogli)*

3 pounds whitefish, sole, or any other lean fish (head and tail removed), cut in 4 portions
5 cups fish stock
3 cups Béchamel Sauce (page 65)
2 tablespoons minced parsley
1 teaspoon basil
1 garlic clove, crushed in a garlic press
4 cups cooked rice
½ cup freshly grated kefalotyri cheese

1. Wrap fish loosely in cheesecloth. Knot the ends. Heat fish stock until boiling. Add fish and simmer until done (about 10 minutes).
2. Remove fish from liquid and discard cheesecloth.
3. Mix Béchamel Sauce with parsley, basil, and garlic.
4. Turn rice into a casserole. Put fish on top. Top with Béchamel Sauce and cheese. Cover tightly with aluminum foil.
5. Set in a 300°F oven 12 to 15 minutes, or until thoroughly heated.

8 servings

Marinated Fish *(Psari Marinata)*

2 pounds halibut, sole, or grouper fillets or fish with heads and tails intact
Salt
Juice of 2 lemons
2 cups flour, seasoned with salt and pepper
Olive oil for frying
½ cup olive oil
¼ cup flour
½ cup white wine
½ cup white wine vinegar
1 can (8 ounces) tomato sauce or 1 cup Tomato Sauce (page 77)
1 teaspoon sugar
1 teaspoon fennel
2 garlic cloves, minced (optional)

1. Season fish with salt and lemon juice. Dip in flour. Heat olive oil in a large skillet; add fish and fry on both sides until medium brown, being careful not to burn the oil.
2. Arrange fish in a baking dish. Discard cooking oil.
3. Combine ½ cup oil and flour in a skillet and, stirring constantly with a wooden spoon, cook until flour browns.
4. Add remaining ingredients and simmer, covered, 15 minutes. Strain over fish. Allow to marinate out of the refrigerator several hours before serving. Adjust salt and pepper. Serve at room temperature or chilled.

6 servings

Vinegar and Oil Dressing with Tomato *(Ladoxido me Domata)*

1 tablespoon imported mustard (Dijon, preferably)
2 tablespoons red wine vinegar, or more to taste
½ cup olive oil
1 large tomato, peeled and diced
2 whole scallions, minced
2 tablespoons minced parsley
1 tablespoon chopped capers
1 teaspoon dill

Put mustard and vinegar into a small bowl. Add olive oil while stirring with a whisk. Add remaining ingredients; mix well. Refrigerate several hours before serving.

1 ¾ cups

Trout in Grapevine Leaves

1 jar (32 ounces) grapevine
    leaves, drained
4 medium trout, cleaned, with
    heads and tails left on
2 tablespoons olive oil
2 tablespoons butter, melted
2 teaspoons oregano
1 teaspoon dill
    Additional oil to brush outside
      of trout
    Salt and pepper to taste
2 lemons, cut in wedges

1. Rinse grapevine leaves thoroughly under cold running water to remove brine.
2. Rinse trout; pat dry.
3. Drizzle 2 tablespoons olive oil and butter in trout cavities. Sprinkle with oregano and dill. Brush oil on outside of fish. Season inside and out with salt and pepper.
4. Wrap each trout in 5 or 6 grapevine leaves. Refrigerate 1 to 2 hours.
5. To charcoal-broil, adjust grill 4 inches from heated coals. Grease a rectangular, long-handled grill on all sides. Place fish in the grill, side by side. Grill one side about 8 minutes, turn, grill until fish flakes easily with a fork (about 8 minutes more).
6. Discard browned outer leaves. Serve trout in remaining leaves. Garnish with lemon wedges.

4 servings

Note: Trout may also be broiled under the broiler. For easy turning, use a long-handled grill.

Sea Chowder

¼ cup olive oil
3 garlic cloves
1 medium onion, quartered
2 bay leaves
    Water to cover fish
1 cup dry white wine
    Juice of 1 lemon
6 squid, cleaned and cut in
    pieces
    Salt and pepper to taste
2 tomatoes, peeled, seeded, and
    diced
3 pounds fish (several kinds),
    skinned and boned
1 pound shrimp, shelled and
    deveined

1. Heat oil in a deep saucepan. Add garlic, onion, and bay leaves. Cook until onion is translucent.
2. Pour in water, wine, and lemon juice. Add squid. Season with salt and pepper. Cover and simmer 40 minutes.
3. Add tomatoes and fish; simmer 8 minutes. Add shrimp; simmer just until shrimp are cooked. Adjust seasonings. Serve at once.

6 servings

Pickled Octopus (Oktapodi Tursi)

1 small octopus (about 2 pounds)
½ cup olive oil
¼ cup white wine vinegar
    Juice of ½ lemon
1 tablespoon minced parsley
½ teaspoon marjoram
    Salt and pepper to taste

1. Beat octopus with the flat side of a metal meat hammer 15 to 20 minutes; it will feel soft and excrete a grayish liquid.
2. Wash octopus thoroughly, drain, and cook in skillet without water until it becomes bright pink. Cut into bite-size pieces.
3. Make a salad dressing of the olive oil, vinegar, lemon juice, parsley, marjoram, salt, and pepper. Mix well.
4. Pour over octopus and store in the refrigerator in a covered container for 5 days before serving.
5. Serve cold as an appetizer.

4 to 6 servings

Steamed Mussels in Wine Sauce (Mithia Krassata)

2 pounds mussels
1 large onion, minced
1 large celery stalk, minced
4 peppercorns
3 cups dry white wine
¼ cup butter (at room temperature)
1 tablespoon flour
1 teaspoon vinegar
1 tablespoon chopped parsley
1 garlic clove
Salt and pepper to taste

1. Scrub mussels well with a vegetable brush and rinse. Put into a kettle with onion, celery, peppercorns, and white wine. Cover and steam until they open, discarding any that are unopened.
2. Put mussels onto a deep platter. Cover and keep warm.
3. Strain liquid and simmer. Mix butter and flour together in a small bowl; stir into hot liquid. Add vinegar, parsley, garlic, salt, and pepper; continue to simmer until liquid is reduced by half.
4. To serve, pour sauce over mussels.

6 servings

Shrimp Giahni with Feta Cheese

1 medium onion, minced
½ cup olive oil
1 can (28 ounces) tomatoes (undrained)
4 ounces white wine
1 small bunch parsley, finely chopped
1 celery stalk, finely chopped
Salt and pepper
1 pound large shrimp, cleaned and deveined
¼ pound feta cheese, crumbled

1. Brown onion in oil. Add tomatoes, stirring until mixture reaches boiling. Lower heat and simmer, covered, 5 minutes. Add wine, parsley, celery, and salt and pepper to taste. Simmer 30 minutes.
2. While tomato sauce is simmering, parboil shrimp 2 minutes in **3 quarts boiling water** with **2 teaspoons salt.** Drain immediately.
3. Add shrimp to sauce. Simmer 1 minute. Garnish with feta.

6 servings

Spiced Shrimp with Onions

4 quarts water
1 tablespoon salt
3 pounds raw shrimp, shelled and deveined
¾ cup white wine vinegar
1 cup olive oil
2 cups white wine
1 tablespoon salt
1 teaspoon pepper
2 jars whole baby onions, drained
3 garlic cloves
1 bay leaf
1 celery stalk, cut in half
Juice of 1 lemon

1. Bring water and 1 tablespoon salt to a rolling boil in a saucepot. Add shrimp. Boil 1 minute. Drain.
2. Combine remaining ingredients in a saucepot and bring to boiling. Simmer uncovered 5 minutes. Cool.
3. Pour onion mixture over shrimp. Refrigerate 6 to 8 hours.
4. Drain shrimp and onions and serve chilled.

6 to 8 servings

Stuffed Squid (Kalamarakia Yemista)

32 squid, cleaned and tentacles removed
¾ cup olive oil
1 large onion, chopped
1½ cups water
1 cup long-grain rice
½ cup chopped parsley
1 teaspoon mint
1 teaspoon basil
2 cloves garlic, crushed in a garlic press
½ cup pine nuts
¼ cup dried black currants
1 cup dry white wine
Salt and pepper to taste
Water
Juice of 2 lemons

1. Reserve squid. Rinse tentacles in cold water. Drain and mince finely.
2. In a large saucepan, heat 2 tablespoons of the oil, add onion and minced tentacles and cook over low heat until tentacles turn pink. Add water. Heat to boiling. Reduce heat, add rice, parsley, mint, basil, garlic, pine nuts, currants, and ½ cup of the wine.
3. Simmer until liquid is absorbed. Season with salt and pepper. Cool.
4. Using a teaspoon, stuff each squid cavity loosely with the rice mixture. Arrange squid in rows in a large baking dish. Combine the remaining wine and olive oil with enough water to reach half the depth of the squid. Season with additional salt and pepper. Cover.
5. Bake at 325°F about 40 minutes, or until squid is tender. Drizzle with lemon juice just before serving.

8 servings

Note: Stuffing may also be used as a side dish. Stuff 16 squid. Put remaining stuffing in a baking dish. Add a little water, salt, and pepper and cover. Bake at 325°F 30 minutes.

Deep-Fried Squid (Kalamarakia Tyganita)

12 squid, cleaned, with their tentacles left on
Flour seasoned generously with salt and pepper
Vegetable oil for deep frying
3 lemons, cut in wedges

1. Rinse the cleaned squid in cold water and pat dry with paper towels. Dip the squid into the seasoned flour and coat all surfaces evenly.
2. Heat the oil in a deep fryer to 375°F. Drop in the squid, a few at a time. Fry until golden brown (about 5 minutes). Transfer the squid with a slotted spoon to a baking dish lined with paper towels. Keep in a 200°F oven until all the squid are fried.
3. Remove paper; serve squid with lemon.

3 servings

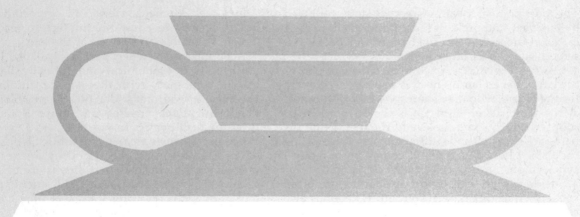

MEAT

The most popular meat in Greece is lamb, followed by kid, veal, and pork. Because it is difficult to raise cattle on Greece's rocky and barren land, beef is not served as often as other meats.

Greek cuisine has a recipe to match every part of the lamb. Baked lamb's head is a specialty reserved for the elders, who may share a morsel with others at the table. Lamb stomach is the basis for tripe soup, to which some cooks add the feet. Lamb innards are chopped and stuffed into a sausage casing for a spicy hors d'oeuvre. Of course, roast lamb is synonymous with Greek Easter.

Suckling pigs, kids, and baby lambs are often cooked whole on an open spit. Shish kebob is also cooked outdoors and is made with lamb.

In Greek kitchens, stews are simmered hours before serving to allow the mixture to reach full flavor. Vegetables are added at the end.

A popular dish, when beef is available, is Beef Soffrito. It is economical and robustly flavored. When combined with homemade hilopites it becomes a gourmet's delight. Lamb Shank in Parchment Paper makes an unusual and picturesque dish perfect for parties.

Greek casseroles are rich and subtle blends, often of meat, sauces, and cheeses. They are served as main courses or, in small portions, as one of several entrées at buffets. Moussaka and Pastichio are the most famous. Their preparation is time-consuming, but the results are worth the effort.

Roast Beef with Wine (Roz Bif)

1 beef rolled rump roast (5 pounds or more)
Salt and pepper
2 garlic cloves, crushed in a garlic press
1 tablespoon oregano
2 tablespoons grated kefalotyri cheese
Chicken stock (about ¾ cup)
1 medium onion, quartered
½ cup red wine
1 package macaroni, cooked according to directions on package
1 cup grated kefalotyri cheese

1. Sprinkle beef roast with salt and generously cover with pepper. Slit the meat with a small sharp knife in several places on a diagonal slant about 1 inch deep.
2. Mix garlic, oregano, and 2 tablespoons cheese. Fill each incision with some of this mixture. Pinch to close incision.
3. Place beef on a trivet in a roasting pan. Pour enough stock into the pan to barely reach top of trivet. Add the quartered onion.
4. Roast at 325°F until done to taste. (A meat thermometer will register 140°F for rare, 160°F for medium, and 170°F for well-done meat.)
5. During the last 15 minutes of roasting, pour in wine.
6. Remove meat to a platter. Keep warm. Remove fat from pan juices. Toss in cooked pasta. Sprinkle with remaining cheese. Serve hot.

About 8 servings

Meatballs with Lemon Sauce (Youverlakia Avgolemono)

2 pounds lean beef, ground
1 large onion, minced
3 tablespoons minced parsley
2 tablespoons mint leaves
½ cup long-grain rice
Salt and pepper to taste
1 garlic clove, crushed in a garlic press
½ cup flour
2 cups water
Salt to taste
2 tablespoons butter
Juice of 1 or 2 lemons
2 eggs, separated

1. Mix thoroughly meat, onion, parsley, mint, rice, salt, pepper, and garlic. Dip hands in flour. Shape meat into round balls about 1 inch in diameter.
2. Bring water and salt to boiling in a large Dutch oven. Add butter and meatballs in a single layer. Simmer covered 40 minutes.
3. Pour stock into a small bowl and add lemon juice. Beat egg yolks until frothy. In another bowl, beat whites until peaks form. Fold in yolks. In a thin stream, pour stock into eggs. Pour over meatballs. Serve hot.

6 servings

Tournedos

6 slices beef loin tenderloin steak
    (1½ inches thick)
  Salt and pepper to taste
½ cup butter
¼ cup flour
¾ cup dry white wine
½ cup chopped parsley
  Juice of 1 lemon

1. Season meat with salt and pepper on both sides.
2. Melt butter in a heavy skillet. Add meat and brown quickly on each side. Remove to a dish.
3. Using a whisk, stir flour into pan juices. Cook, stirring constantly, over low heat for 2 minutes.
4. Stir in wine and cover. Simmer 5 minutes.
5. Add meat, parsley, and lemon juice. Simmer 5 minutes.

6 servings

Braised Beef Corfu Style *(Soffrito)*

3 cups all-purpose flour
  Salt and pepper to taste
1 teaspoon paprika
  Olive oil for frying
4 pounds beef round top round,
    cut in slices ¼ inch thick or
    less
4 garlic cloves, crushed in a
    garlic press
1 cup red wine vinegar
1½ cups water
1 teaspoon sugar
1 bay leaf
¼ cup chopped parsley

1. Season flour with salt, pepper, and paprika.
2. Heat olive oil in a skillet. Lightly dip meat slices in flour. Shake off excess. Brown meat on each side in the olive oil. Arrange in a casserole.
3. Combine garlic, vinegar, water, sugar, bay leaf, and parsley in a small saucepan; heat to boiling. Pour over the meat.
4. Bake at 325°F 1 hour, or until the meat is tender and almost all the liquid is absorbed.
5. Serve with **mashed potatoes.**

About 8 servings

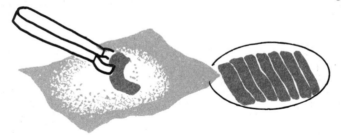

Beef Stew with Lentils or Lima Beans

5 pounds beef chuck roast
¼ cup olive oil
2 large onions, thinly sliced
4 celery stalks, chopped
2 large carrots, chopped
1½ pounds fresh tomatoes, peeled
    and diced
2 parsley sprigs, minced
1 pound dried lentils (or lima
    beans)
  Salt and pepper to taste
3 garlic cloves, crushed in a
    garlic press
1 cup dry red wine
3 cups beef stock (or more if
    necessary)

1. Trim excess fat from beef roast. Cut meat into large cubes.
2. Heat oil in a large Dutch oven. Brown meat on all sides and remove to platter.
3. Put onions into the Dutch oven and cook until translucent. Pour off excess fat.
4. Return meat to the Dutch oven. Arrange vegetables, parsley, and lentils around the meat. Season with salt and pepper.
5. Combine garlic, wine, and stock in a saucepan. Bring to boiling. Pour over meat and vegetables. Cover. Simmer until meat is tender. (Meat should be covered with liquid throughout cooking.)

8 to 10 servings

Note: This dish is tastier when made early and allowed to rest several hours or overnight, then reheated.

Beef with Baby Onions *(Stifatho)*

¼ cup olive oil
4 pounds beef shoulder, cut in large pieces
Salt and pepper to taste
1 can (16 ounces) tomatoes (undrained)
1 tablespoon tomato paste mixed with ½ cup water
5 garlic cloves, crushed in a garlic press
1 cup red wine
1 teaspoon sugar
1 tablespoon lemon juice
1 bay leaf
Pinch cinnamon
1 teaspoon oregano
¼ cup chopped parsley
3 tablespoons pickling spice (put in a tea infuser or wrapped and securely tied in cheesecloth)
3 pounds whole fresh baby onions, peeled

1. Heat oil in a large Dutch oven. Brown meat well on all sides. Season with salt and pepper.
2. Add tomatoes and diluted tomato paste. Cover and simmer 10 minutes.
3. Add remaining ingredients, except onions. Cover. Bring to a boil. Reduce heat. Simmer 2 to 3 hours until meat is tender.
4. Meanwhile, cut a small cross at the base of each onion. During the last ½ hour of cooking, add onions. Adjust salt and pepper.
5. Serve with **rice** or **pasta**.

8 servings

Moussaka

Fried Eggplant:
3 medium eggplants
Salt
2 cups flour (about)
Olive oil combined with vegetable oil for frying

Meat Filling:
¼ cup butter
2 pounds lean beef or lamb, ground
1 large onion, minced
¼ cup minced parsley
1½ teaspoons tomato paste mixed with ½ cup water
½ cup dry white wine
Salt and pepper to taste
3 egg whites, beaten until stiff
6 tablespoons fine bread crumbs

Béchamel Sauce with Egg Yolks:
7 tablespoons butter
7 tablespoons flour
1½ quarts milk, scalded
3 egg yolks, beaten
1 cup grated kefalotyri cheese

1. Slice eggplants ¼ inch thick, and place on a large platter in a single layer. Sprinkle with salt on both sides. Let stand at least 30 minutes, or until liquid beads form on surfaces. Take each slice, squeeze well between both hands or press down with a heavy weight, being sure all liquid is squeezed out.
2. Dip each slice lightly in flour. Shake off excess. Heat oil in a large skillet. Fry eggplant, turning once, until golden brown. Drain on paper towels. Set aside.
3. For Meat Filling, melt butter in a large skillet; add meat and onion, and cook until browned. Add parsley, tomato paste and water, wine, salt, and pepper. Cook until all liquid has evaporated (about 30 minutes). Cool.
4. Beat egg whites until they form soft mounds. Fold in half the bread crumbs. Fold egg-white mixture into meat mixture.
5. For Béchamel Sauce, heat butter until melted. Stir in flour. Cook 4 minutes over low heat, stirring constantly; do not brown. Pour in warm milk slowly. Cook over low heat until sauce thickens. Cool. Stir in yolks with a whisk.
6. To assemble, oil an 18x12-inch baking pan. Dust with remaining bread crumbs. Line bottom of pan with 1 layer of eggplant. Cover with meat. Layer remaining eggplant on top. Sprinkle with cheese. Pour Béchamel Sauce over.
7. Bake at 350°F about 40 minutes, or until golden brown. Cool. Cut into squares and serve.

About 10 servings

Pastichio

3 tablespoons olive oil
2 pounds ground beef or lamb
1 large onion, grated
  Few parsley sprigs, chopped
1 tablespoon tomato paste mixed
  with ½ cup water
1 pound elbow macaroni, cooked
  according to directions on
  package and drained
1 pound fresh kefalotyri cheese,
  grated

Béchamel Sauce:
½ cup butter, melted
7 tablespoons flour
1½ quarts milk, heated to
  lukewarm
10 eggs, separated

1. Heat oil in a large skillet. Add meat and onion and cook until meat is brown. Add chopped parsley and diluted tomato paste. Cover and simmer for 30 minutes. If any liquid remains, cook meat uncovered until liquid has evaporated.
2. Spread half the cooked macaroni in an 18x12-inch baking dish and cover with all the meat mixture. Sprinkle top with three fourths of the cheese. Form a layer with remaining macaroni.
3. Meanwhile, to make sauce, melt butter in a large saucepan. Add flour and mix with a whisk for several minutes. Gradually add milk while stirring; simmer until sauce thickens, stirring frequently.
4. Separate eggs. Beat whites in a bowl until they pile softly. Beat yolks in another bowl. Fold yolks and whites together, then fold in sauce. Spoon over meat and macaroni. Sprinkle with remaining cheese.
5. Bake at 325°F about 45 minutes, or until golden brown. Cool slightly before serving.

8 servings

Note: Pastichio may be prepared and baked in advance. To reheat, cover tightly with foil and heat in a 200°F oven.

Meatballs with Tomato Sauce *(Giouverlakia me Domata)*

1 pound beef, freshly ground
1 large onion, minced
3 tablespoons long-grain rice
1 garlic clove
½ cup minced parsley
1 tablespoon basil
  Salt and pepper to taste
1 cup flour for rolling
  Olive oil for frying
2 tablespoons tomato paste
  mixed with 1 cup water or
  beef stock

1. In a large bowl, combine meat, onion, rice, garlic, parsley, basil, salt, and pepper. Dip hands in flour. Shape meat mixture into round balls about 1½ inches in diameter.
2. Heat oil in a skillet. Sauté the meatballs, turning to brown on all sides. Remove to a baking dish.
3. Pour tomato paste liquid into the skillet. Simmer 3 minutes, stirring and scraping constantly. Strain the juices over the meatballs and add as much water or beef stock as needed to half cover them. Loosely cover with foil.
4. Bake at 350°F about 40 minutes. Once or twice during the cooking, turn meatballs with a wooden spoon. Serve hot with **pilafi** or **mashed potatoes.**

About 6 servings

Sautéed Sweetbreads *(Glykathia Tyganita)*

4 pairs sweetbreads from
  milk-fed calves
  Ice water
2 teaspoons salt
1 tablespoon lemon juice
5 tablespoons butter or olive oil
  for frying
  Flour seasoned with salt and
  pepper

1. Soak sweetbreads in ice water mixed with salt for 1 hour. Drain.
2. Place sweetbreads in boiling water to cover. Add lemon juice and simmer 10 minutes. Drain. Plunge at once into ice water. Remove membranes and connective tissue, and split into 2 pieces.
3. Melt butter or heat olive oil in a skillet. Dip sweetbreads into flour. Fry until golden brown on all sides.

2 servings

Stuffed Grapevine Leaves with Egg and Lemon Sauce
(Dolmathes Avgolemono)

1 jar (32 ounces) grapevine leaves
1 quart water
¼ cup butter
2 medium onions, minced
1 pound ground lean beef or lamb or a combination of the two
Salt and pepper to taste
2 tablespoons mint
2 tablespoons minced parsley
½ cup long-grain rice
2½ cups lukewarm water or more to barely cover dolmathes
4 egg yolks
½ cup lemon juice

1. Rinse grapevine leaves thoroughly in cold running water to remove brine. Bring 1 quart water to boiling. Add the leaves and parboil 3 minutes. Strain. Select 4 to 6 coarse, large leaves and line the bottom of a Dutch oven with them.

2. For filling, melt butter in a skillet. Add onion and cook until translucent. Remove from heat. Add meat, salt, pepper, mint, parsley, and rice. Toss lightly with 2 forks.

3. To fill, place a leaf, glossy side down, with the stem pointing toward you. (If a leaf is too small, use 2, overlapping 1 over the other by ¾ inch.) Place 2 teaspoons filling just above where the stem begins. Tuck base up and over. To seal, loosely fold one side, then the other, over toward the middle. Roll up to form oblong rolls, leaving room for the rice to expand while cooking.

4. To cook, arrange the dolmathes side by side in Dutch oven, layer upon layer. Place a ceramic plate on the last layer to keep dolmathes from floating to the surface during cooking. Pour water into pan to cover dolmathes. Cover pot and simmer 50 to 60 minutes. Check occasionally to see if too much water has evaporated. Add a little at a time, if necessary.

5. To make sauce, beat egg yolks until frothy. While continuing to beat, add lemon juice, a tablespoon at a time. Drain 1 cup broth from the cooked dolmathes and add slowly to the egg mixture, beating constantly.

6. Remove plate from dolmathes. Pour egg and lemon sauce over. Set over low heat until hot; do not boil. Serve immediately.

20 to 30 dolmathes

Tomatoes Stuffed with Meat and Rice
(Domates Yemistes me Kimake Rizi)

12 large firm tomatoes
1 teaspoon sugar
½ teaspoon salt
¾ cup olive oil
2 onions, minced
1 garlic clove, crushed in a garlic press
1 pound lean ground beef or lamb
¼ cup long-grain rice
¼ cup chopped parsley
1 teaspoon mint
½ teaspoon cinnamon
Salt and pepper to taste
½ cup water

1. Slice tops from tomatoes and save. Remove pulp and save. Sprinkle insides of tomatoes with sugar and salt.

2. Heat ¼ cup oil in a large skillet. Add onion and garlic and sauté until onion is translucent. Add meat and cook until no longer red. Add rice, seasonings, and tomato pulp. Simmer 10 minutes. Cool slightly.

3. Fill tomatoes two thirds full, leaving room for rice to expand. (If too much filling is added, tomatoes may break open.) Place in a baking dish. Put tops on tomatoes. Drizzle remaining olive oil between tomatoes. Add ½ cup water.

4. Bake at 350°F about 40 minutes, or until rice is tender, basting occasionally. (Add more liquid to dish, if necessary.)

12 servings

Stuffed Peppers: Follow recipe for Tomatoes Stuffed with Meat and Rice, substituting **green peppers** for tomatoes. Remove seeds from peppers and discard. Proceed as directed.

Roast Leg of Lamb with Orzo *(Ghiouvetsi)*

1 lamb leg (6½ to 7 pounds)
4 large garlic cloves, peeled and
    cut in half lengthwise
¼ cup oregano, crushed
1 tablespoon salt
2 tablespoons freshly ground
    pepper
    Juice of 2 lemons
1 pound orzo (a pasta)
¼ cup cooking oil
1 tablespoon salt
1 cup boiling water
2 medium onions, quartered
¾ cup shredded or grated
    kefalotyri cheese

1. First prepare the lamb by placing it on a large sheet of aluminum foil. With a small, sharp knife, make eight 1-inch-deep diagonal incisions on the top and bottom the lamb. Into each incision, insert half a garlic clove. Press meat back to cover incisions.
2. Combine oregano, 1 tablespoon salt, and the pepper. Rub this all over the lamb. Fold the four sides of foil up to form a cuff. Pour on lemon juice. Seal the foil and refrigerate at least 6 hours, or preferably overnight.
3. Place leg of lamb on a rack in a roasting pan.
4. Roast in a 450°F oven 20 minutes. Turn oven control to 350°F. Roast until meat is cooked as desired; a meat thermometer inserted in the leg will register 160°F for medium and 170°F to 180°F for well-done meat.
5. Remove from roasting pan to a carving board. Keep warm. When ready to serve, slice meat on the diagonal. Save the pan drippings to use for making gravy.
6. Prepare orzo by boiling it according to directions on the package, adding cooking oil and 1 tablespoon salt. Drain. Rinse under hot water.
7. To make gravy for the orzo, remove the fat from the pan drippings. Add boiling water while stirring with a spoon to loosen drippings on bottom of the pan. Add onions.
8. Bake at 350°F 15 minutes.
9. Pour the gravy with onions into a blender and purée. Return to the roasting pan. Combine the orzo with the gravy. Toss quickly. Serve with shredded kefalotyri as an accompaniment to the lamb.

6 to 8 servings

Saddle of Lamb with Artichoke Purée

1 (5 pounds) saddle of lamb
    (lamb loin roast)
2 tablespoons olive oil
    Salt and pepper
2 teaspoons oregano
4 garlic cloves, crushed in a
    garlic press
8 to 10 thick grapevine leaves
8 artichoke bottoms, cooked
1 pound mushrooms, cooked
2 tablespoons butter
½ cup red wine
½ cup water

1. Rub lamb with olive oil. Combine salt, pepper, oregano, and garlic. Rub over lamb. Cover with grapevine leaves. Seal with foil. Refrigerate overnight.
2. Purée artichoke bottoms and mushrooms. Combine with butter and heat.
3. Set roast in a roasting pan. Remove grapevine leaves and season with salt and pepper.
4. Roast in a 325°F oven 50 minutes. Remove from oven. Reserve juices in the pan. Separate each loin from the saddle in one piece. Cut the meat into slices. Spread each slice with some of the purée. Reassemble the loins and tie securely in place. Return the meat to the roasting pan and add wine and water. Continue roasting, basting frequently, for 15 minutes.
5. Remove to a serving platter and discard strings. Skim fat from the pan juices and strain juices over the meat.

About 10 servings

Lamb Shank in Parchment Paper

1 lamb shank per serving
For each serving:
  1 garlic clove, peeled and
      slivered
  1 slice hard mizithra cheese
  1 small onion, sliced
  1 small tomato, peeled and diced
  1 teaspoon minced parsley
  ¼ teaspoon dill
  ¼ teaspoon mint flakes
  ½ teaspoon oregano
      Juice of ½ lemon
      Salt and pepper to taste
  1 teaspoon olive oil
      Parchment paper
      Cotton string

1. Make several incisions in the meat, top and bottom. Insert sliver of garlic in each incision.
2. Place meat on a piece of parchment paper ample enough to seal meat and vegetables securely. Put cheese on meat, then arrange onion and tomato on top. Sprinkle with herbs, lemon juice, salt, and pepper. Drizzle with olive oil.
3. Wrap securely in parchment paper. Tie with string. Set in a roasting pan.
4. Bake at 350°F about 1½ hours, or until meat is done. Serve package unopened.

Note: Oiled brown paper may be substituted for the parchment paper.

Braised Lamb Shanks

  3 tablespoons olive oil
  6 lamb shanks
      Salt and pepper to taste
  1 can (16 ounces) tomatoes
      (undrained)
  2 cups red wine
  ¼ cup dried oregano
  2 bay leaves
  ¼ cup minced parsley
  2 garlic cloves, minced
  2 onions, quartered

1. Heat olive oil until it begins to smoke. Brown lamb shanks on all sides. Season with salt and pepper. Add tomatoes, wine, oregano, bay leaves, parsley, garlic, and onion. Cover. Simmer 2 to 2½ hours, or until meat is fork tender.
2. Remove from heat. Cool. Skim off fat. Reheat and serve hot.

6 servings

Lamb with Endive Avgolemono *(Arni me Antithia Avgolemono)*

  3 large bunches curly endive
  1 quart water
  3 tablespoons olive oil
  5 pounds lamb shoulder with
      bone, cut in large pieces
  1 medium onion, minced
  2 tablespoons flour
  2 cups water
      Salt and pepper to taste
  3 eggs
      Juice of 2 lemons

1. Wash endive thoroughly under running cold water to remove grit. Cut off coarse stems. Bring 1 quart water to boiling in a large saucepot. Remove from heat and add endive. Let stand 3 minutes. Drain.
2. Heat olive oil in a large Dutch oven. Add meat and brown on all sides. Add onion. Cover and simmer, stirring occasionally.
3. Combine flour with 2 cups water in a bowl; stir well. Pour into meat. Season with salt and pepper. Add endive, cover, and continue cooking 1½ to 2 hours, or until meat is tender. (There should be enough stock for avgolemono sauce.)
4. To prepare sauce, beat eggs in a bowl and, beating constantly with a whisk, add lemon juice in a steady stream. Take 1 cup stock from meat and add, a tablespoon at a time, beating constantly.
5. Pour sauce over meat and endive. Heat; do not boil.

6 servings

Lamb Shish Kebob *(Arni Souvlakia)*

¾ cup dry red wine
¼ cup lemon juice
3 tablespoons olive oil
1 teaspoon salt
  Freshly ground pepper to taste
2 garlic cloves, crushed in a
    garlic press
1 onion, minced
  Bay leaf
2 tablespoons oregano, crushed
3 pounds leg of lamb, boneless,
    cut in 1½-inch cubes
  Green peppers, cored and cut
    in squares
  Baby onions, peeled and left
    whole
  Large mushroom caps
  Tomato wedges

1. Make a marinade of wine, lemon juice, olive oil, salt, pepper, garlic, onion, bay leaf, and oregano in a large bowl and add lamb cubes. Cover securely and refrigerate at least 6 hours. Turn lamb several times while marinating.
2. Remove meat from marinade and place on skewers with green pepper squares, onions, mushroom caps, and tomato wedges.
3. Barbecue over hot coals or broil about 20 minutes, or until done; baste with marinade during cooking.

8 to 10 servings

Lamb Stew with Eggplant *(Arni me Melitzana)*

2 pounds lean lamb shoulder, cut
    in large pieces
1 cup flour seasoned with salt
    and pepper
2 tablespoons olive oil
1 large onion, minced
3 large tomatoes, peeled and
    diced
¾ cup water
1 bay leaf
  Salt and pepper to taste
3 cups water
2 medium eggplants, cut in large
    cubes
2 garlic cloves, crushed in a
    garlic press
1 tablespoon tomato paste

1. Dip lamb lightly in flour.
2. Heat oil in a large skillet. Add meat and brown on all sides. Remove meat with a slotted spoon.
3. Put onion in the oil and sauté until translucent.
4. Return meat to skillet. Add tomatoes, water, and bay leaf. Season with salt and pepper. Bring to boiling. Reduce heat and simmer, covered, for 1½ hours.
5. Meanwhile, bring water to a boil in a saucepan. Add eggplant and simmer 5 minutes (to remove bitter taste). Pour off water.
6. Add eggplant, garlic, and tomato paste to meat. Stir to blend. Cover. Simmer about 40 minutes, or until meat is tender.

4 to 6 servings

Lamb Chops with Oregano *(Kotolettes Arniou me Rigani)*

2 lamb chops (rib or loin) per
    serving

For each serving:
1 tablespoon oregano
  Salt to taste
1 lemon, cut in half
1 tablespoon olive oil (optional)
  Pepper to taste

1. An hour before cooking, sprinkle lamb chops with oregano. Season with salt. Set aside.
2. Place lamb chops on a broiler rack and broil 7 minutes on each side.
3. Remove from broiler and squeeze lemon juice over the chops. Drizzle with oil. Season with pepper.

Lamb-Stuffed Zucchini with Avgolemono Sauce

8 medium straight zucchini
1 pound ground beef round or
 lamb
½ cup long-grain rice
1 small onion, minced
2 tablespoons chopped parsley
1 teaspoon chopped mint
 Salt and pepper
 Water (about 2 cups)

Sauce:
 2 egg yolks
 Juice of 2 lemons
 ½ cup broth

1. Remove the ends and scrape the skins of the zucchini. With a corer, scoop out the zucchini centers and discard. Soak the zucchini in cold water.
2. Meanwhile, mix meat with rice, onion, parsley, mint, salt, and pepper. Drain zucchini and stuff with meat mixture.
3. Arrange stuffed zucchini in a single layer in a Dutch oven. Add enough water to half cover the zucchini. Bring the water to a boil, reduce heat, and simmer, covered, about 35 minutes.
4. Before serving, beat egg yolks until frothy. Slowly add lemon juice, beating constantly. Add broth, tablespoon by tablespoon, beating constantly. Heat thoroughly, but do not boil. Pour over zucchini. Serve immediately.

4 servings

Roast Baby Lamb's Head *(Arni Kefalaki Psito)*

1 head per serving, split in half
 and tied with a string to
 keep brains intact
 Juice of 1 lemon
2 tablespoons olive oil
1 tablespoon oregano or more to
 taste
 Salt and pepper to taste

1. Soak head in cold salted water for 1 hour. Drain. Pat dry. Cut string and place halves in a shallow pan, brains up.
2. Combine lemon juice, olive oil, oregano, salt, and pepper. Drizzle over head.
3. Roast in a 350°F oven for about 20 minutes, basting frequently until brains are tender. Remove brains with a spoon and keep warm. Continue roasting about 45 minutes more, or until other parts are tender.

Lamb Kidneys in Wine Sauce *(Nefra Krasata)*

4 lamb kidneys
 Water
1 tablespoon wine vinegar
3 tablespoons flour
¼ cup butter
1½ cups white wine
1 bay leaf
1 garlic clove
2 tablespoons minced parsley
2 teaspoons oregano
½ teaspoon cumin
 Salt and pepper to taste

1. Soak kidneys in cold water and vinegar for 15 minutes. Drain. Remove opaque skin and cut out the core. Slice kidneys thinly.
2. Dip slices in flour.
3. Melt butter in a skillet. Sauté the kidneys until browned on both sides. Add wine, bay leaf, garlic, parsley, oregano, cumin, salt, and pepper. Cover and simmer 20 minutes.

4 servings

Steamed Mussels in Wine Sauce, 53;
Deep-Fried Squid, 54;
Charcoal-Grilled Fish, 49

Shepherdess' Pie *(Pita tys Voskopoulas)*

1½ cups Béchamel Sauce
1 medium onion, minced
1 egg, beaten
¼ cup fresh cracker crumbs
¼ cup chopped parsley
1 teaspoon salt
1 teaspoon thyme
¼ teaspoon ground red pepper
1 teaspoon vinegar
1 pound coarsely ground lamb or lean beef
4 cups mashed potatoes
½ cup grated kefalotyri cheese
1 teaspoon paprika

1. Combine ¾ cup of Béchamel Sauce, onion, egg, cracker crumbs, parsley, salt, thyme, red pepper, and vinegar.
2. Combine sauce with meat, tossing with 2 forks to mix lightly. Spoon mixture into a baking dish. Level top lightly with the back of the spoon. Make an indentation in the center.
3. Bake at 350°F 30 minutes, removing fat as it collects in the indentation.
4. Combine potatoes with remaining sauce.
5. Remove meat from oven when done. Sprinkle with cheese. Cover with potatoes. Sprinkle with paprika. Bake 20 minutes.

4 servings

Béchamel Sauce: Melt ¼ **cup butter.** Whisk in **3 tablespoons flour.** Cook, stirring constantly, for 1 minute. Slowly pour in **1½ cups milk,** scalded. Cook, stirring constantly, until mixture coats a wooden spoon.

Charcoal-Roasted Pig *(Gourounipoulo tys Skaras)*

3 garlic cloves, crushed in a garlic press
2 cups dry white wine
Juice of 2 lemons
1 tablespoon salt
¼ cup oregano
2 tablespoons crushed peppercorns
1 piglet (12 to 15 pounds), with eyes, tongue, and feet removed
½ cup olive oil
1 tablespoon paprika

1. Make a marinade by combining garlic, wine, lemon juice, salt, oregano, and peppercorns. Refrigerate 1 hour.
2. Score pig several places with a knife. Rub interior cavity and exterior surface with marinade. Allow to marinate 12 hours in refrigerator.
3. Crush aluminum foil into a firm, thick ball and put in mouth to keep open. Cover ears with foil so they will not burn. Pull front feet forward and tie together. Pull hind feet backwards and tie together. Cover feet loosely with foil.
4. Attach pig to revolving spit and roast, basting frequently with a mixture of oil and paprika, until skin is brown and crisp and meat is tender (about 5 hours). In the last hour, remove foil so ears and feet can brown.
5. Remove pig from spit. Set on a platter. Put an apple or other piece of fruit in its mouth. Pour off fat from pan juices and serve.

8 to 10 servings

Pork Chops with Vegetables

3 tablespoons vegetable oil
8 lean pork chops
1 can (15 ounces) stewed tomatoes
1¾ cups water
1 cup minced celery
1 large green pepper, minced
1 medium onion, minced
1 bay leaf
1 thyme sprig
¼ teaspoon paprika
Salt and pepper to taste

1. Heat oil in a large deep skillet. Add chops and brown on both sides.
2. Turn stewed tomatoes into a bowl. Add water, celery, green pepper, onion, bay leaf, thyme, paprika, salt, and pepper; mix well.
3. Remove excess fat from skillet; add tomato mixture. Cover.
4. Bake at 325°F about 2 hours, or until tender. Serve pork chops with **pilafi** or **potatoes.** Pass gravy separately.

8 servings

Pastichio, 59; Braised Beef Corfu Style, 57; Lamb Shish Kebob, 63

Pork Braised with Celery in Egg and Lemon Sauce
(Hoirino Selin Avgolemono)

¼ cup butter
4 pounds lean pork, cut in 2-inch cubes
1 large onion, minced
2 cups water
2 bunches celery (stalks only), cut in 1-inch pieces

Avgolemono Sauce:
¼ cup butter
3 tablespoons flour
2 cups pork stock
Juice of 2 lemons
3 eggs, separated
Salt and pepper to taste

1. Melt butter in a Dutch oven and sauté pork until golden brown. Add onion and cook until translucent. Add water. Cover and simmer 1 to 1½ hours, or until meat is just tender. Add celery and simmer about 15 minutes, or until tender. Drain off 2 cups stock and strain. Keep meat warm.
2. To make sauce, melt butter in a saucepan; add flour and cook about 1 minute, stirring constantly; do not brown. Add pork stock and lemon juice. Simmer, stirring constantly, until sauce thickens.
3. Separate eggs. Beat whites until soft peaks form. Beat yolks until thick. Fold yolks into whites. Using a wire whisk, slowly add sauce to eggs. Pour over pork mixture. Heat and serve at once.

8 servings

Pork Sausage with Orange Peel (Loukanika)

2 pounds pork shoulder, ground
½ pound pork fat back, ground
Grated peel of 1 navel orange
2 garlic cloves, crushed in a garlic press
1 tablespoon minced parsley
1 tablespoon oregano
2 teaspoons salt
2 teaspoons anise seed
2 teaspoons coriander, ground
1½ teaspoons allspice, ground
1 teaspoon pepper
1 long casing, cut in 7- to 8-inch pieces

1. Combine pork shoulder, fat back, and remaining ingredients, except casings, in a bowl and mix thoroughly. Cover and refrigerate several hours.
2. Rinse casings thoroughly in lukewarm water. Tie one end of a casing and stuff by pushing meat through a funnel inserted in the untied end; tie other end. Continue until all the meat and casings have been used.
3. Poach sausages in boiling water for 1 hour. Cool. Cut into slices and fry in a skillet until browned.

Note: If desired, omit casing, form sausage into patties, and fry until cooked.

Roast Veal

3 pounds veal rump roast, boned, rolled, and tied
1 garlic clove
1 tablespoon dill
1 teaspoon oregano
Salt and pepper to taste
3 tablespoons butter
¼ cup water
¼ cup white wine
1 teaspoon rosemary

1. Rub roast with garlic, dill, and oregano. Season with salt and pepper.
2. Melt butter in a roasting pan. Brown veal well on all sides.
3. Place a rack under veal. Pour water and wine into bottom of pan. Add rosemary. Cover pan.
4. Roast in a 350°F oven 2 hours.
5. Serve with pan juices.

6 to 8 servings

Sautéed Veal Brains in Browned Butter *(Myala Tyganita)*

4 veal brains
Juice of 2 lemons
1 teaspoon salt
½ cup flour seasoned with salt
   and pepper
½ cup butter
2 tablespoons chopped fresh dill
1 lemon, cut in wedges

1. Rinse brains thoroughly. Soak in water with ice cubes for 15 minutes. Drain; remove membranes.
2. Pour enough water into a saucepot to cover brains. Add lemon juice and salt; bring to boiling. Reduce heat and drop in brains. Simmer 15 minutes. Drain. Plunge into ice water to cool quickly.
3. Dip brains into seasoned flour.
4. Put butter into a skillet and heat until deep brown. Add brains and sauté briefly. Remove to a warm platter. Sprinkle with dill. Serve with lemon wedges.

4 servings

Braised Veal with Lemon and Anchovies

6 thick slices veal shin, sawed
   through so marrow shows
½ cup flour
½ cup butter
1 cup dry white wine
¼ cup chicken or veal stock
1 can (16 ounces) tomatoes
   (undrained)
2 teaspoons salt
1 teaspoon ground pepper
1 teaspoon thyme
2 garlic cloves, crushed in a garlic
   press
1 teaspoon grated lemon peel
½ cup minced parsley
2 anchovies, minced

1. Roll veal shin slices lightly in flour.
2. Melt butter in a Dutch oven and add veal, browning on all sides. Add wine, stock, tomatoes, salt, pepper, thyme, and garlic. Cover. Simmer about 2 hours, or until meat is tender, adding a little liquid when necessary.
3. Sprinkle with lemon peel, parsley, and anchovies before serving.

3 servings

Cypriote Sausages

1 pound coarsely ground beef
1 pound coarsely ground pork
1 cup fresh bread crumbs
3 garlic cloves, crushed in a
   garlic press
2 teaspoons salt
2 teaspoons coriander
1 teaspoon cumin
1 teaspoon thyme
½ teaspoon paprika
¼ teaspoon ground red pepper
1 bay leaf, ground
1 egg
½ cup minced parsley
1 large onion, minced
2 tablespoons tomato paste
   mixed with ½ cup water
Flour for rolling
Oil for frying

1. Combine meats in a large bowl, tossing with 2 forks.
2. Combine remaining ingredients except flour and oil in a separate bowl. Toss with meat mixture.
3. Break off enough meat to form a 2-inch-long sausage. Lightly flour palms of hands. Roll meat into sausage shapes.
4. Heat oil to smoking in a skillet. Fry sausages until deep brown on all sides. Serve hot or cold.

20 to 30 sausages

Veal Stew with Onions (Moskari Stifatho)

Flour seasoned with salt,
    pepper, and paprika
6 veal shanks, cut in pieces
3 tablespoons olive oil
3 tomatoes, peeled, seeded, and
    cubed
2 tablespoons chopped parsley
1 cup water
1 tablespoon wine vinegar
2 garlic cloves, minced
1 teaspoon sugar
1 bay leaf
2 whole cloves
2 whole allspice
    Pinch red pepper seed
2 pounds whole baby onions
    Water

1. Put seasoned flour into a bag. Add shank pieces and shake to coat evenly.
2. Heat oil in a Dutch oven and brown meat on all sides. Add tomatoes, parsley, 1 cup water, wine vinegar, garlic, and sugar. Tie bay leaf, cloves, allspice, and red pepper seed in cheesecloth. Add to meat mixture. Cover and simmer 1 hour.
3. Meanwhile, peel onions. Cut a small cross on the bottom of each. Add to stew and pour in enough water to cover. Simmer until onions are tender (about 25 minutes). Discard spices. Serve hot with **rice** or **cracked wheat pilafi.**

3 or 4 servings

Rabbit Stew (Kounelli Stifatho)

2 rabbits, skinned, cleaned, and
    cut in four pieces each
1½ cups mild vinegar
1 cup water
1 large onion, quartered
2 teaspoons salt
1 teaspoon pepper
2 bay leaves
2 pounds whole baby onions
3 tablespoons olive oil
2 tablespoons tomato paste
    mixed with 1 cup water
1 cup red wine
1 garlic clove, crushed in a garlic
    press
1 bay leaf
⅛ teaspoon cinnamon
    Salt and pepper to taste
    Water to cover

1. Put rabbit pieces into a large bowl. Add vinegar, water, onion, salt, pepper, and bay leaves. Cover. Refrigerate 24 hours, turning occasionally. Pat dry.
2. Peel onions. Cut a small cross at the base of each (to keep onions whole during cooking).
3. Heat olive oil in a large Dutch oven and sear rabbit on all sides until reddened. Add all ingredients including onions and water to barely cover. Bring to a boil. Cover.
4. Bake at 250°F about 2 hours, or until rabbit is tender.

8 servings

Note: If a thick sauce is desired, pour the sauce into a saucepan and simmer uncovered for ½ hour. Pour over rabbit.

POULTRY

In Greece, chickens are omnipresent. There are few homes in Greek villages and towns whose yards do not have one or more chickens strutting about. A frequent sight in warm weather is a bus going down a dusty road from one village to another with crates of squawking hens tied to the roof.

Older, fatter chickens are used for making stock and stews. Younger ones are used for broiling or simmering with vegetables.

Many chicken recipes are generations old and have been handed down by grandmothers through the years. Kotopoulo Vorthonia is named for a village in Sparta. Vegetables and cheese are popular ingredients in chicken recipes.

Chicken with Tomatoes and Onions *(Kotopoulo Riganati)*

2 broiler-fryer chickens
3 tablespoons olive oil
Juice of 1 lemon
2 teaspoons salt
½ cup butter
1 can (20 ounces) tomatoes (undrained)
1 teaspoon pepper
1 tablespoon oregano
Salt

1. Rinse chickens well and pat dry with paper towels. Rub inside and out with a mixture of olive oil, lemon juice, and 2 teaspoons salt. Place in a large roasting pan.
2. Bake at 375°F 1 hour.
3. Melt butter in a saucepan. Add tomatoes, pepper, and oregano. Simmer 5 minutes.
4. Pour sauce over the chickens. Turn oven heat to 325°F and bake chickens an additional 45 minutes; baste frequently. Salt to taste.

4 servings

Note: Kotopoulo Riganati freezes very well.

Chicken and Grapes

6 tablespoons butter
2 broiler-fryer chickens, cut in pieces
Salt and pepper to taste
3 scallions, chopped
1 cup dry white wine
Clusters of seedless white grapes
½ teaspoon paprika

1. Melt butter in a skillet. Add chicken and brown. Season with salt and pepper. Transfer chicken to a casserole.
2. Add scallions to the skillet and cook until browned. Add wine and heat. Pour over the chicken. Cover.
3. Bake at 350°F 30 minutes. Remove cover. Add grapes and bake an additional 5 minutes. Sprinkle with paprika.

4 to 6 servings

Braised Chicken with Tomatoes and Cheese
(Kotopoulo Vorthonia)

1 chicken (3 pounds), cut in
   small pieces
¼ cup olive oil
   Salt and pepper to taste
1 can (16 ounces) tomatoes
   (undrained)
1 medium onion, minced
1 garlic clove, crushed in a garlic
   press
2 tablespoons oregano
¼ teaspoon cinnamon
2 tablespoons whiskey
1 pound orzo (a pasta)
¼ cup vegetable oil
1 cup grated hard mizithra
   cheese

1. Rinse chicken and pat dry with paper towels.
2. Heat olive oil in a large skillet. Add chicken pieces. Season with salt and pepper. Brown on all sides.
3. Mash tomatoes and add to skillet. Add onion, garlic, oregano, cinnamon, and whiskey. Cover and simmer about 30 minutes, or until done. Remove chicken pieces and keep hot.
4. Cook orzo according to directions on the package, adding vegetable oil to the water. Drain thoroughly and put into a deep serving dish. Add the sauce and toss lightly until orzo is coated completely. Adjust seasoning. Add the chicken. Toss again to combine.
5. Serve with grated cheese.

6 to 8 servings

Chicken Breasts with Yogurt Sauce
(Kotopoulo me Saltsa Yaourti)

½ cup butter
6 chicken breasts, boned
   Salt and pepper to taste
½ teaspoon paprika
6 fresh scallions, chopped
¼ cup minced parsley
2 cups chicken stock
   Juice of 1 lemon
1 pound mushrooms, sliced
2 cups plain yogurt
1 cup coarsely ground walnuts

1. Melt butter in a large skillet. Add chicken and season with salt, pepper, and paprika. Brown on both sides.
2. Add scallions, parsley, chicken stock, and lemon juice; bring to a boil. Reduce heat and simmer covered about 20 minutes, or until chicken is tender.
3. Remove chicken and arrange on a serving platter.
4. Add mushrooms to the stock. Simmer uncovered 3 minutes. Blend in yogurt and walnuts. (If sauce is too thick, dilute with a little stock or water.) Heat just to warm yogurt; do not boil.
5. Pour sauce over chicken.

6 servings

Broiled Chicken in Lemon Juice and Oregano
(Kotopoulo me Lemoni ke Rigani)

2 broiler-fryer chickens, cut up
½ cup olive oil
Juice of 2 lemons
¼ cup oregano, crushed
Salt and pepper to taste

1. Rinse chicken pieces and pat dry.
2. In a bowl, make a marinade by combining olive oil with lemon juice and oregano. Dip each piece of chicken into the marinade. Season with salt and pepper. Marinate for several hours, or overnight if possible.
3. In a preheated broiler, place the chicken fleshy side down. Broil about 6 inches from heat about 15 minutes, or until brown, basting frequently. Turn once. Broil until done.

4 servings

Note: The marinade may be served as a gravy with cooked rice or noodles.

Roast Chicken with Potatoes
(Kotopoulo tou Fournou me Patates)

1 chicken (about 4 pounds)
Salt and pepper to taste
Juice of 1 lemon
¼ cup butter
¼ teaspoon paprika
1 cup water
5 medium potatoes, pared

1. Season chicken, inside and out, with salt, pepper, lemon juice, butter, and paprika. Place chicken on a rack in a baking dish.
2. Bake at 350°F about 1¼ hours, or until chicken is tender, basting occasionally. After the first 30 minutes of cooking, pour in water; add potatoes and baste with drippings.
3. Turn oven control to 400°F. Remove chicken to a platter and keep warm. Turn potatoes over in dish. Bake an additional 5 to 10 minutes.

5 servings

Rock Cornish Hens with Oranges and Almonds

1 Rock Cornish hen per serving

For each serving:
2 tablespoons butter, melted
2 tablespoons orange juice
Salt and pepper to taste
¼ teaspoon marjoram
¼ teaspoon thyme
½ garlic clove, crushed in a garlic press
½ navel orange with peel, cut in thin slices
2 tablespoons honey (about)
5 almonds, blanched, slivered, and toasted

1. Rinse hen well. Drain and pat dry. Place in a shallow baking dish. Drizzle inside and out with butter.
2. Combine orange juice, salt, pepper, marjoram, thyme, and garlic in a small bowl. Pour over and into the bird. Marinate 2 hours; turn occasionally.
3. Set bird on a broiler rack and put under broiler about 6 inches from heat. Broil 12 minutes on each side, or until tender, basting frequently with the marinade. During the last few minutes of broiling, arrange orange slices around the bird and drizzle with honey.
4. Garnish with almonds and serve at once.

Chicken in Filo *(Kotopita)*

1 stewing chicken, cut in pieces
½ cup unsalted butter
1 medium onion, minced
½ cup finely chopped leek
1 celery stalk, minced
1 garlic clove, crushed in a garlic press
2 tablespoons finely chopped parsley
2 tablespoons pine nuts
3 tablespoons flour
2½ cups chicken stock
½ cup cream
4 eggs, beaten until frothy
¼ teaspoon nutmeg
½ teaspoon dill
2 tablespoons white wine
Salt and pepper
1 package filo
Additional butter for filo

1. Rinse chicken pieces. In a large heavy Dutch oven, add ¼ cup butter. When hot, add the chicken. Cover. Cook, turning, without browning, for about 15 minutes.
2. Remove the chicken pieces and cool slightly. Remove bones and skin from chicken and discard. Chop chicken meat. Set aside.
3. Melt 2 tablespoons butter in a skillet. Add onion, leek, celery, garlic, parsley, and pine nuts. Sauté until vegetables are limp.
4. Melt remaining butter in a saucepan and blend in flour. Cook 2 minutes. Stir in stock. Simmer until sauce boils. Cool. Stir in cream, eggs, nutmeg, dill, chicken, vegetables, and wine, if sauce seems too thick. Season with salt and pepper.
5. Butter a 12x9x3-inch baking pan. Line it with 6 sheets of filo, brushing each with butter, following directions on pages 80-81.
6. Spread chicken filling evenly over filo. Top with filo according to directions.
7. Bake at 350°F about 50 minutes, or until golden in color. Let stand 15 minutes before cutting into squares. Serve warm.

8 to 10 servings

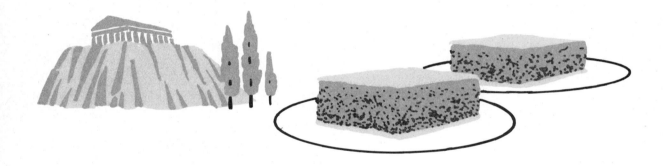

Chicken with Cheese *(Kotopoulo me Tyri)*

¼ cup butter
1 chicken (3 pounds), cut in pieces
1 medium onion, minced
Salt and pepper to taste
½ teaspoon rosemary
¼ teaspoon paprika
1 garlic clove, crushed in a garlic press
1½ cups chicken broth
⅓ pound kasseri cheese, cut in thin slices

1. Melt butter in a large skillet. Brown chicken on all sides. Add onion. Season with salt and pepper. Add rosemary, paprika, garlic, and chicken broth. Simmer, covered, about 40 minutes, or until chicken is tender.
2. Lay cheese slices on top of chicken. Simmer, covered, 5 minutes more. Serve at once.

2 to 4 servings

Stuffing for a Small Turkey (Yemisi yra Galopoulo)

½ cup butter
1 onion, minced
1 medium cooking apple, pared, cored, and diced
1 pound mushrooms, sliced
2 medium potatoes, boiled, peeled, and diced
½ cup pine nuts
½ cup dried black currants
1 cup blanched almonds, sliced
2 pounds chestnuts, boiled and cleaned
4 cups prepared bread stuffing
2 cups or more chicken stock to make a moist stuffing
1 can (4½ ounces) pâté de foie gras
Salt and pepper to taste

1. Melt butter in a large deep skillet. Add onion, apple, and mushrooms; cook until tender.
2. Add potatoes, pine nuts, currants, almonds, chestnuts, stuffing, and stock. Heat thoroughly over low heat, adding more liquid if necessary.
3. Stir in pâté. Season with salt and pepper.
4. Cool completely. Stuff bird.

Stuffing for a small turkey or 2 capons

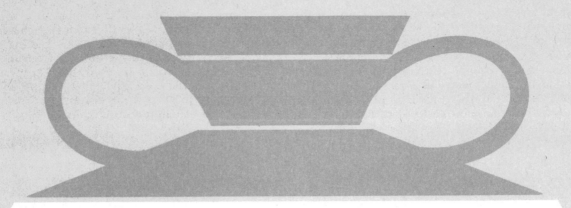

PASTA AND RICE

Greeks are so fond of pasta, potatoes, and semolina foods that it is difficult to decide which is the most popular. Throwing dietary caution to the winds, cooks often serve two starches at one meal.

Pilaf made from rice or cracked wheat accompanied by yogurt provides a tart accent for meat and poultry. Potatoes browned in pan juices are another favorite addition to a meal.

Semolina, a coarsely ground meal made from wheat, is the main ingredient for homemade noodles. Sometimes called "farina," semolina should not be confused with the breakfast cereal.

Orzo, occasionally referred to as "manestra," is a small seed-shaped pasta that can be added to soups and to roast-meat dishes. It is featured in Roast Leg of Lamb with Orzo (page 61).

Pasta with Fresh Tomatoes and Artichoke Hearts

For each serving:
- 1 medium ripe tomato, peeled, seeded, and diced
- 2 cooked artichoke hearts, cut in half
- 1 teaspoon oregano
- ½ teaspoon basil
- 1 garlic clove, crushed in a garlic press
- Salt and pepper to taste
- 1 tablespoon wine vinegar
- 3 tablespoons olive oil
- ½ cup macaroni, cooked according to package directions
- Mizithra cheese, cut in slices, for garnish
- Kalamata olives for garnish

1. Combine all ingredients except macaroni and garnishes in a bowl. Cover and marinate several hours.
2. Turn macaroni onto a plate. Cover with marinated mixture. Garnish with cheese and olives. Serve cool.

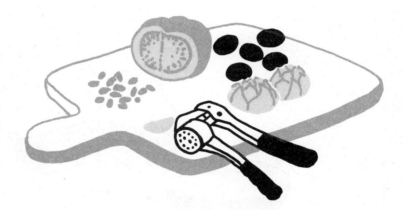

Spaghetti Timbale

- 2 tablespoons oil
- 1 medium onion, minced
- 2 tomatoes, peeled and coarsely chopped, or ½ cup drained canned Italian-style tomatoes
- Salt and pepper to taste
- 2 tablespoons chopped fresh parsley
- 1 package (16 ounces) spaghetti
- 2 tablespoons oil
- 4 eggs, lightly beaten with a fork
- ¾ cup freshly grated mizithra cheese
- 3 tablespoons butter
- 1 cup cubed salami or Pork Sausage with Orange Peel (page 66)

1. Heat 2 tablespoons oil in a heavy saucepan. Cook onion over low heat until translucent. Add tomatoes, salt, and pepper, stirring often, until mixture thickens. Stir in parsley.
2. Cook spaghetti according to package directions; add 2 tablespoons oil to water.
3. Toss cooked spaghetti with eggs, cheese, salt, and pepper until thoroughly mixed.
4. Butter a baking dish with some of the butter. Add a layer of half the spaghetti and a layer of salami; spoon the tomato sauce over. Cover with spaghetti and dot with remaining butter.
5. Bake at 300°F 20 minutes.

6 servings

Macaroni with Sausage *(Makaronatha me Loukanika)*

2 pounds Pork Sausage with
    Orange Peel (page 66)
1 garlic clove, sliced
1 large onion, minced
1 can (24 ounces) tomato sauce or
    3 cups Tomato Sauce, heated
Salt and pepper to taste
1 teaspoon oregano
1 tablespoon chopped parsley
½ cup water
1 package (16 ounces) macaroni
½ to ¾ cup grated kefalotyri
    cheese

1. Pull off sausage casings.
2. Brown meat in a large skillet. Add garlic and onion, cook until lightly browned. Discard fat. Add tomato sauce, salt, pepper, oregano, parsley, and water; cover. Simmer over low heat 30 minutes.
3. Boil macaroni according to directions on the package; drain. Put macaroni into a serving dish and cover with sauce. Sprinkle with cheese. Serve hot.

6 to 8 servings

Tomato Sauce *(Saltsa me Domates)*

3 tablespoons butter
1 large onion, chopped
2 pounds fresh ripe tomatoes,
    peeled and chopped
2 teaspoons sugar
2 whole cloves
1 bay leaf
1 garlic clove, crushed in a garlic
    press
1 teaspoon vinegar
Salt and pepper to taste

Melt butter in a saucepan; add onion and cook until translucent. Add tomatoes and remaining ingredients. Simmer uncovered 20 minutes.

3 cups

Note: A variation served during Lent is Anchovy Tomato Sauce. To prepare, use **olive oil** instead of butter, decrease sugar to 1 teaspoon, increase vinegar to 2 teaspoons; and add **½ tube anchovy paste** or **1 can (2 ounces) anchovies**, drained and cut into small pieces.

Macaroni in Browned Butter with Grated Cheese
(Makaronatha me Voutero ke Kefalotyri)

1 pound macaroni
1 cup butter
½ cup freshly grated kefalotyri or
    Parmesan cheese (or more to
    taste)

1. Cook macaroni according to directions on the package, adding ¼ **cup cooking oil** and **1 tablespoon salt.** Drain. Rinse under hot water.
2. Brown butter in a saucepan, stirring constantly.
3. Return the macaroni to the pot in which it was cooked, or place it in a warm serving dish. Drizzle the browned butter over it. With two spoons lift the macaroni to coat all the strands evenly. Cover with freshly grated kefalotyri. Serve at once.

4 to 6 servings

Cracked Wheat Pilafi *(Pligouri)*

3 tablespoons butter
1¼ cups cracked wheat
3 cups stock, heated
Salt and pepper to taste

Melt butter in a large saucepan, add wheat, and cook over low heat, tossing lightly with a fork until lightly browned. Add stock, cover, and simmer about 30 minutes until wheat is done. Season with salt and pepper.

4 servings

Homemade Noodles *(Hilopites)*

3 cups semolina
3 eggs
3 tablespoons olive oil (do not substitute)
1½ teaspoons salt
1½ teaspoons warm water

1. Combine all ingredients in a mixing bowl and work with fingers until dough holds together and can be shaped into a ball. A few drops of water may be added, if necessary, but do not let dough get sticky.
2. Knead dough on a board until smooth and shiny. Cover and let rest 15 minutes. Divide dough into 4 portions. Roll out each portion into a paper-thin sheet.
3. Lay sheets on a linen cloth and allow to dry for 1 to 2 hours.
4. Loosely fold sheets over jelly-roll fashion. Cut strips no more than ¼ inch wide. Holding in place, cut again at right angles, the same width, to make square noodles. Hilopites may be cooked right away or dried.
5. To dry, transfer to a large tray, and spread on a linen surface for about 3 days, turning occasionally.
6. To cook, bring a large quantity of water, with **salt** and **2 tablespoons oil** added, to a rolling boil. Add noodles and boil until they have doubled in size (about 5 minutes).
7. Serve hot with **browned butter** or **tomato sauce.** Sprinkle with **grated kefalotyri cheese.**

About 2 pounds noodles

Rice with Pine Nuts *(Pilafi me Koukounaria)*

¼ cup butter
1 small onion, minced
4 cups rice, cooked in chicken broth
¼ cup pine nuts
Juice of 1 lemon
1 teaspoon dill
½ teaspoon mint
Salt and pepper to taste

Melt butter in a saucepan. Add onion and sauté until translucent. Add cooked rice, pine nuts, lemon juice, dill, mint, salt, and pepper. Heat thoroughly.

6 servings

Rice in Tomato Sauce *(Pilafi me Domata)*

½ cup canned tomato sauce
1½ cups water
¼ cup butter
1 small onion, minced
Juice of 1 lemon
1 cup long-grain rice
Salt and pepper to taste

In a saucepan, combine tomato sauce, water, butter, onion, and lemon juice. Simmer covered until butter is melted. Add rice. Continue simmering until the liquid is absorbed (about 20 minutes). Season with salt and pepper.

4 to 6 servings

FILO

that it lies flat on one piece of the foil, and cover it with the other. Remove one sheet at a time. With the filo unrolled, it is then relatively simple to count the number of leaves in order to estimate if there is a sufficient quantity for the recipe. Cautious cooks always buy a backup package to ensure a sufficient number of leaves.

Greek Easter Bread, 30;
Roast Leg of Lamb with Orzo, 61

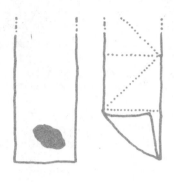

With all materials—warm, melted butter or olive oil and fillings, as well as a pastry brush and a sharp knife or single-edged razor blade—ready to be put to use quickly, uncover the filo, laying out a sheet at a time. For such things as Spanakopeta, Galatobouriko, or Baklava, the filo should be placed in the pan and buttered or oiled with the pastry brush according to the recipe. For recipes calling for soft, liquid fillings, allow the filo to overhang the pan by an inch. After the filling has been poured in, flip the overhanging filo onto the filling. Proceed with layering in this manner until all the filo has been used. Score the topmost leaves into serving-size pieces in diamonds or squares, as desired.

The ever-popular pites are made by cutting a filo into strips 1½ to 2 inches wide. Put about 1 teaspoon of the filling 1 inch above the base of the strip. Fold the filo over the filling, taking the lower left-hand corner and bringing it up to a point diagonally opposite it, creating a small triangle. Then, take the lower right-hand corner and fold it straight up. Again create a small triangle, this time by folding diagonally across from the right-hand side. Then take the left-hand corner and fold it straight up. Continue, creating the triangles and folding from bottom to top until the entire strip of filo is enfolded.

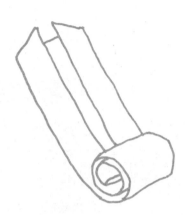

For pasties (trigonopitakia), cut a filo strip about 3 inches wide. Place a dollop of filling about 1½ inches in diameter so that it rests 1½ inches above the base, centered between the edges of the filo strip. Fold each side of the filo strip in toward the filling for the entire length of the strip. Fold the 1½-inch piece up from the base so that it just covers the filling. Roll upward until the entire filo is folded over.

Feta Cheese Triangles *(Tyropites)*

1 pound feta cheese, crumbled
2 egg yolks
1 whole egg
3 tablespoons chopped parsley
   Dash finely ground pepper
¾ pound butter, melted and kept warm
1 pound filo

1. Mash feta cheese with a fork. Add egg yolks, egg, parsley, and pepper.
2. Melt butter in a saucepan. Keep warm, but do not allow to brown.
3. Lay a sheet of filo on a large cutting board. Brush with melted butter. Cut into strips about 1½ to 2 inches wide. See pages 80-81 for how to handle filo. Place ½ teaspoon of the cheese mixture on each strip about 1 inch from base. Fold to form a triangle. Continue until all cheese mixture and filo have been used.
4. Place triangles, side by side, in a shallow roasting pan or baking sheet.*
5. Bake at 350°F about 20 minutes, or until golden brown. Serve at once.

About 100 pieces

Note: Tyropites freeze well. Before serving, remove from freezer and let stand 15 to 20 minutes. Bake at 325°F until golden brown.

*Pan must have four joined sides; otherwise butter will fall to bottom of the oven and burn.

Koulourakia I, 91; Baklava, 84; Pasta Flora, 88

Meat Pasties *(Trigonopitakia me Kima)*

3 tablespoons butter, melted
1 pound lean ground beef
1 medium onion, finely chopped
2 tablespoons tomato sauce
½ cup dry white wine
   Salt and pepper to taste
1 tablespoon minced parsley
1 tablespoon mint
1 cup crumbled feta cheese
1 egg, beaten
2 teaspoons cracker meal
1 package filo
   Butter for filo

1. Melt butter in a skillet. Add beef, onion, tomato sauce, wine, salt, pepper, parsley, and mint. Cook over low heat, stirring frequently until all liquid evaporates. Cool.
2. Add cheese, egg, and cracker meal to meat mixture; stir to mix.
3. See pages 80-81 for how to handle filo.
4. Arrange the pasties in a shallow baking pan.
5. Bake at 350°F about 15 minutes, or until golden brown. Serve hot.

50 to 100 pieces depending on size

Meat Pie Ioannina *(Kreatopita Yianniotiki)*

½ cup butter, melted
2 pounds ground lean lamb
1 large onion, chopped
2 scallions, chopped
2 tablespoons tomato paste
   mixed with 1 cup wine
   Salt and pepper to taste
½ teaspoon cinnamon or more to
   taste
¼ cup chopped parsley
2 cups fresh bread crumbs
½ cups milk
1½ cups stock
7 eggs, separated
¾ cup grated kefalotyri cheese
1 package filo or 2 double recipes
   of pie crust
   Butter, melted and kept warm,
   or equal parts olive oil and
   vegetable oil

1. Melt butter in a large skillet. Add meat, onion, and scallions, and cook until browned, stirring occasionally. Add tomato paste with wine, salt, pepper, cinnamon, and parsley; mix well. Cover. Simmer 20 minutes.
2. Toss bread crumbs with milk and stock. Stir into meat mixture.
3. Beat egg whites in a bowl to form soft peaks. Beat yolks in another bowl until thick. Fold yolks into whites. Mix in cheese. Set aside.
4. Line bottom and sides of a 12x9-inch baking pan with 4 filo leaves. (See pages 80-81 for how to handle filo.) Spread with the meat filling. Cover with egg and cheese mixture. Top with remaining filo sheets. Score the top 2 or 3 filo sheets in squares, using a sharp knife. If using pie crust, prick with a fork.
5. Bake at 350°F 40 minutes. Let stand 15 minutes before cutting.

10 to 12 servings

Kefalonian Meat Pie *(Kreatopita Kefalonias)*

¼ cup butter
2 pounds lean lamb, cut in
   1-inch cubes
2 cups lamb stock or water
½ pound feta cheese, crumbled
1 large onion, chopped
4 medium potatoes, parboiled,
   peeled, and diced
1 tablespoon olive oil
¼ cup chopped parsley
1 teaspoon grated orange peel
1 garlic clove, crushed in a garlic
   press
2 teaspoons dill
½ teaspoon cinnamon
   Salt and pepper
4 hard-cooked eggs, sliced
1 package filo
   Butter, melted and kept warm
   without browning

1. Melt butter in a skillet, add meat, and brown lightly on all sides. Pour in lamb stock and simmer covered about 20 minutes, or until meat is just tender. Remove from heat. Cool. Add cheese, onion, potatoes, oil, parsley, orange peel, garlic, dill, cinnamon, salt, and pepper; mix well. Set aside.
2. Place 1 sheet of filo in a 12x9-inch baking dish, allowing the filo to hang over the dish a little on all sides. Lightly butter filo. (See pages 80-81 for how to handle filo.) Repeat 4 times. Pour filling evenly in the pan. Arrange sliced eggs over the filling. Adjust salt and pepper. Flip the edges of filo onto the filling. Cover with remaining filo. Score the top 2 or 3 filo sheets in squares with a sharp knife.
3. Bake at 325°F about 1 hour, or until filo is golden brown.

10 to 12 servings

Note: Pie crust can be substituted for filo. Use a double recipe. Prick top crust with a fork.

Trigona with Walnuts *(Trigona me Karithia)*

Syrup:
2 cups honey
3 cups water
2 cups sugar
½ cinnamon stick

Filling:
2 cups walnuts
1 jigger cognac
1 cup sugar
1 teaspoon cinnamon
½ cup cracker meal
1 cup unsalted butter, melted
   and kept warm
1 pound filo (some may be left
   over)

1. For syrup, combine all ingredients in a saucepan. Bring to a boil. Reduce heat, cover, and simmer 20 minutes. Cool to lukewarm.
2. For filling, grind walnuts until the texture of cornmeal. Add liquor, sugar, cinnamon, and cracker meal; mix into a ball. If mixture is too dry, add water, a teaspoon at a time, mixing well.
3. Lay a sheet of filo on a large cutting board. Brush with melted butter. Cut into strips about 1½ to 2 inches wide. (See pages 80-81 for how to handle filo.) Place 1 teaspoon of the nut mixture on each strip about 1 inch from base. Fold to form a triangle. Continue until all nut mixture and filo have been used.
4. Put Trigona in a shallow baking pan.* Brush tops with butter.
5. Bake at 350°F about 20 minutes, or until golden in color. Cool 2 minutes. Dip in lukewarm syrup. Serve at room temperature.

30 to 50 pieces depending on size

*Pan must have four joined sides; otherwise butter will fall to bottom of the oven and burn.

Baklava

Syrup:
2 cups honey
2 cups sugar
3 cups water
2 whole cloves
1 stick cinnamon

Filling:
2 pounds chopped walnuts or
   blanched almonds
1 tablespoon cinnamon

Filo:
¾ pound unsalted butter, melted
2 packages filo

1. For syrup, combine all the ingredients in a large saucepan. Bring to a boil. Lower heat at once, cover, and simmer for 20 minutes. Remove from heat and cool to room temperature.
2. For filling, combine walnuts and cinnamon in a bowl. Set aside.
3. For filo, melt butter in a saucepan, being careful not to let it brown. Reheat it if it cools and does not spread easily.
4. Remove the layers of filo from their plastic wrapper and lay them flat on a large sheet of aluminum foil. Cover with another sheet of foil. (Filo must be kept completely covered at all times or it will dry out.)
5. Separate the filo layers one at a time. Brush with butter the bottom and sides of an 18x12-inch baking pan. Line the bottom of the pan with 4 filo layers, brushing each layer with melted butter before adding the next. After the fourth filo layer has been buttered, sprinkle it evenly with one third of the chopped nuts. Add 2 more filo layers, buttering each. Sprinkle with the remainder of the nuts. Cover with remaining filo, buttering each layer.
6. With a very sharp knife or a single-edge razor blade, using a ruler as a guide, cut into the topmost layers, tracing diamond shapes by making vertical cuts from one end of the pan to the other 1 inch apart, and diagonal cuts slightly less than ½ inch apart.
7. Bake at 250°F 1 hour and 50 minutes, or until golden. Cool 5 minutes. Pour the cooled syrup over it. Let stand overnight so syrup can be completely absorbed. Using a sharp knife, cut through each piece completely.
8. Remove the baklava slices with a fork to paper cupcake cups. Store no more than several weeks at room temperature. Baklava does not retain its crispness if stored in the refrigerator.

50 to 60 pieces

Galatobouriko

Syrup:
2 cups water
½ cup honey
1 cup sugar
½ stick cinnamon
1 whole clove
   Grated peel of ½ lemon

Filling:
1 quart milk
½ cup sugar
½ cup unsalted butter
½ cup semolina
6 eggs
1 teaspoon vanilla extract

Filo:
1½ packages filo
½ pound unsalted butter, melted

1. For syrup, combine all ingredients in a large saucepan. Bring to a boil. Lower heat, cover, and simmer 20 minutes. Remove from heat and cool.
2. For filling, combine milk and sugar in a deep saucepan. Heat over low heat until scalded. Do not allow mixture to boil. Add butter and stir until melted. Add semolina in a steady stream, stirring with a whisk to prevent lumps. Cook until mixture begins to thicken.
3. Beat eggs until frothy. Fold into cooked milk mixture.
4. To prepare filo, see directions on pages 80-81. Layer filo and filling in a 12x9-inch baking pan, using 10 filo sheets per layer. Cover with remaining filo.
5. Bake at 325°F about 45 minutes, or until golden brown. Let Galatobouriko stand 5 minutes before pouring syrup on it. Set aside for 6 hours before serving.

12 servings

DESSERTS

Greeks usually end their meals with fruit, and during the nut-harvesting season, some freshly picked nuts are added. During the walnut-harvesting season, on the Ionian island of Lefkas, hostesses offer guests small plates of walnut halves in honey.

The rich desserts for which Greeks are famous—Baklava, Galatobouriko, Kataifi, and Diples—are reserved for special occasions. These are baked for family ceremonies, when guests are expected, as presents to give during a visit, and for the various religious holidays.

Diples, along with a sterling silver or gold coin, are given to new mothers to wish them and their newborn a sweet life and physical strength as strong as the coin.

Kourambiethes, always served at weddings, are also featured at other gala happenings.

A Greek cook's pantry always has Loukoumi, Koulourakia, and Paximathia on hand for an unexpected caller.

Figs with Mavrodaphne Wine *(Syka me Mavrodaphne Krasi)*

12 ripe figs
2 cups Mavrodaphne wine
2 cups whipping cream, whipped
¼ cup walnuts

1. Peel figs. Prick each 3 or 4 times on sides and bottoms. Arrange figs in a dish and pour wine over them. Refrigerate for 2 hours, turning occasionally.
2. Remove figs to a serving platter. Reserve the wine. Arrange whipping cream around the figs. Garnish with walnuts. Serve wine separately.

4 servings

Whole Wheat Porridge with Currants and Almonds *(Kourkourti)*

5 cups whole wheat
Water
Salt, sugar, and cinnamon
1 cup coarsely ground blanched almonds
½ cup dried currants (optional)

1. Place whole wheat in a large saucepan. Cover with cold water and let stand overnight.
2. The next day, drain wheat. Cover with fresh cold water. Simmer about 4 hours, or until tender, stirring frequently to prevent scorching and adding water as needed. Stock will become very thick.
3. Drain wheat stock into a saucepan. Add salt, sugar, and cinnamon to taste. Stir in almonds, currants, and 1 cup of the boiled wheat, if desired. Serve hot.

4 servings

Revani

1 cup unsalted butter
½ cup sugar
1 teaspoon grated lemon or orange peel
5 eggs
2 cups semolina
1 cup flour
1 tablespoon baking powder
Syrup:
3 cups sugar
1 quart water
1 cinnamon stick

1. Cream butter with sugar and grated peel. Beat together 5 minutes. Add eggs, one at a time, beating until well blended after each.
2. Combine semolina, flour, and baking powder. Add to creamed mixture and mix together by hand. Spread in a buttered 9-inch square pan.
3. Bake at 350°F 40 to 45 minutes. Cool 5 minutes.
4. While Revani is baking, prepare the syrup. Combine sugar, water, and cinnamon. Bring to boiling, reduce heat at once, and simmer covered 20 minutes.
5. Pour syrup over cake. Cool, then slice into squares. Serve plain or garnished with **whipped cream** and **toasted almonds** or accompanied with **fresh fruit.**

10 to 12 servings

Drop Yeast Doughnuts *(Loukoumathes)*

2 packages active dry yeast
2 cups warm water (105° to 115°F)
3 to 4 cups all-purpose flour
1 teaspoon salt
  Vegetable oil or olive oil or a combination of the two for deep frying
  Honey and cinnamon

1. Dissolve yeast in 1 cup warm water in a small bowl.
2. Add 1½ cups flour to yeast. Beat batter with a wooden spoon until smooth.
3. Cover with a towel and put into a warm place until batter is double in bulk.
4. Pour into a larger bowl, add remaining water, salt, and flour to make a thick but runny batter.
5. Cover with a towel and put into a warm place until batter is double in bulk and begins to bubble.
6. Half fill a deep fryer with oil. Heat just until smoking.
7. Drop batter by tablespoonfuls into oil; occasionally dip spoon in oil before dipping in batter. Cook until golden brown. Remove with a slotted spoon.
8. Drizzle with honey and sprinkle with cinnamon. Serve hot.

About 30

Diples

2 eggs
1 egg yolk
1 tablespoon butter, melted
  Grated peel of 1 orange (optional)
¼ cup orange juice
2 tablespoons lemon juice
  Semolina (about 2½ cups)
½ teaspoon baking powder
½ teaspoon salt
  Oil for deep frying (4 to 5 inches deep)
  Honey
  Cinnamon
  Chopped walnuts

1. Beat eggs and egg yolk until fluffy. Add melted butter, grated peel, orange juice, and lemon juice.
2. Mix 1 cup semolina with baking powder and salt. Stir into egg mixture. Add another cup semolina and mix well. Add remaining ½ cup semolina as necessary to make a soft dough. It will be a little sticky. Knead on a board until elastic and smooth.
3. Divide dough into 3 portions. Lightly flour a large board and roll dough as thin as for noodles. Using a sharp knife, cut dough into 4-inch-wide strips. Cover dough until ready to fry.
4. Heat oil in a deep saucepan. When oil reaches 350°F, regulate temperature and drop in a piece of dough. Using two forks, turn in one end and roll up quickly to the other. Remove with a slotted spoon as soon as light gold in color. Drain on absorbent towels.
5. To serve, pour warm honey over the Diples and sprinkle with cinnamon and walnuts.

About 4 to 5 dozen

Shredded Wheat Nut Dessert *(Kataifi)*

3 cups sugar
1 quart water
  Grated peel of 1 lemon
2 whole cloves
4 cups walnuts, coarsely ground
½ cup sugar
2 teaspoons cinnamon
2 pounds kataifi dough
1½ cups unsalted butter, melted
1 tablespoon rosewater

1. Combine 3 cups sugar, water, peel, and cloves in a saucepan. Bring to a boil. Reduce heat, cover, and simmer 20 minutes. Set aside to cool.
2. Combine nuts, ½ cup sugar, and cinnamon in a bowl. Set aside.
3. Take enough kataifi dough to pat into a 4x3-inch flat piece. Put 1 tablespoon of the nut filling in the center, fold dough over, and shape into a roll. Continue until all the filling and dough have been used.
4. Place rolls, 1 inch apart, in a greased large baking pan. Spoon melted butter over each roll.
5. Bake at 325°F about 40 minutes, or until golden brown. Remove from oven and sprinkle with rosewater. Pour cooled syrup over. Cool several hours before serving.

About 30

New Year's Day Cake *(Vasilopita)*

3½ cups all-purpose flour
2 teaspoons baking powder
1 cup softened unsalted butter
1 cup sugar
2 eggs (at room temperature)
1 egg yolk
   Grated peel of 1 orange
¼ teaspoon nutmeg (optional)
¼ cup cream
1 tablespoon cognac
1 silver coin, boiled and wrapped
   in foil
   Blanched almonds (about 20)
1 egg white, beaten until frothy

1. Sift flour and baking powder; set aside.
2. Using an electric mixer, beat butter until fluffy. Add sugar gradually, beating 4 minutes. Add eggs and egg yolk, one at a time, beating after each. Add peel and nutmeg. Combine cream and cognac; add gradually while beating.
3. Add dry ingredients, using a wooden spoon to mix in well. Stir in coin.
4. Heavily grease a 10-inch round cake pan. Turn batter into pan. Press edge with fork tines to decorate. Arrange blanched almonds in a decorative pattern on top.
5. Bake at 350°F 15 to 20 minutes, or until cake is set. Pull out from oven, brush with egg white, and return to oven. Continue baking until a wooden pick inserted in the center comes out clean (about 20 minutes). Cool before serving.

8 to 10 servings

Walnut Honey Cake *(Karithopeta)*

Syrup:
1 cup sugar
½ cup honey
1 cup water
1 teaspoon lemon juice
1 cinnamon stick

Cake:
¾ cup unsalted butter (at room
   temperature)
½ teaspoon grated orange peel
¾ cup sugar
3 eggs
1 cup all-purpose flour
1½ teaspoons baking powder
½ teaspoon cinnamon
¼ teaspoon salt
¼ cup milk
1 cup chopped walnuts

1. For syrup, bring all ingredients to a boil in a saucepan. Simmer 20 minutes. Set aside to cool.
2. For cake, cream butter, orange peel, and sugar together until fluffy. Beat in eggs, one at a time, beating well after each addition.
3. Mix flour, baking powder, cinnamon, and salt. Fold flour mixture into butter mixture, alternating with milk. Stir in nuts.
4. Pour batter into a greased and floured 8-inch square pan.
5. Bake at 350°F 30 minutes, or until done.
6. Remove cake from oven, cool, and cut into diamonds while in the pan.
7. Pour syrup over cake. Cool. Refrigerate and let soak 24 hours before serving.

2 to 3 dozen

Pasta Flora

½ cup unsalted butter (at room
   temperature)
2 eggs
1 teaspoon vanilla extract
1 cup sugar
3 cups all-purpose flour
1 tablespoon baking powder
1 pint jam or preserves
1 egg yolk, beaten with ½
   teaspoon water

1. Beat butter 4 minutes, using an electric mixer. Add eggs, vanilla extract, and sugar. Beat until fluffy. Mix flour and baking powder. Slowly work into mixture until well blended.
2. Divide dough into 2 parts; one a ball using three fourths of the total, and one using one fourth of the total.
3. Line the bottom a 13x9-inch baking pan with the larger portion of the dough. Spread the preserves evenly over dough.
4. Roll the remaining quarter of the dough on a lightly floured board to fit the size of the pan. Cut into strips. Form a lattice over the preserves. Brush dough with the egg yolk and water.
5. Bake at 350°F about 45 minutes until pastry is golden brown or a wooden pick comes out clean when inserted. Cool. Cut into squares.

10 servings

Copenhagen Pita (Copenhai)

Syrup:
3 cups sugar
1½ cups honey
5 cups water
½ stick cinnamon

Cake:
1½ cups butter
1 cup confectioners' sugar
5 eggs
1½ cups flour
1 tablespoon baking powder
2 tablespoons cognac

Filling:
5 eggs
2 cups sugar
1 teaspoon cinnamon
3 pieces zwieback, ground
1½ cups almonds, blanched and ground

Topping:
1 package filo
1½ cups butter

1. For syrup, combine sugar, honey, water, and cinnamon in a large saucepan. Bring to boiling. Reduce heat and simmer 20 minutes. Set aside to cool.
2. For cake, cream butter and confectioners' sugar. Add eggs, one at a time, beating well after each. Mix flour and baking powder and add to butter mixture. Add cognac and mix well.
3. Spread mixture evenly in a greased 18x12-inch baking pan. Set aside.
4. For filling, separate eggs. Beat yolks slightly, add sugar, and beat until light and fluffy.
5. Beat egg whites in another bowl until stiff, not dry, peaks are formed. Fold whites into yolk mixture. Combine cinnamon, zwieback crumbs, and almonds and fold into egg mixture. Spread evenly over layer in pan.
6. For topping, layer 10 sheets of filo over top, buttering after each layer has been added; see pages 80-81 for how to handle filo. Drizzle a little butter over top layer. Score topmost sheets into diamond shapes.
7. Bake at 350°F about 50 minutes, or until golden in color. Remove from oven and pour cooled syrup over.
8. Let stand several hours before serving.

About 60 pieces

Turkish Delight (Loukoumi)

2 cups granulated sugar
½ cup light corn syrup
½ cup cornstarch plus 3 tablespoons extra for dusting
3 cups water
1 tablespoon rosewater
⅛ teaspoon ground mastic
2 tablespoons fresh lemon juice
¾ cup unsalted pistachios
Confectioners' sugar for rolling

1. Combine granulated sugar and corn syrup in a saucepan and bring to boiling, stirring constantly. Cook for 30 seconds. Cool.
2. In another saucepan, combine ½ cup cornstarch with water. Simmer mixture until thick. Mix cornstarch into syrup and bring slowly to boiling. Stir to prevent lumps from forming. Reduce heat to very low and cook uncovered, stirring occasionally, until a candy thermometer registers 220°F. Stir in rosewater, mastic, lemon juice, and pistachios.
3. Pour the hot mixture into a square pan lined on bottom and sides with a heavy cotton cloth dusted with cornstarch. Spread mixture and dust top with cornstarch. Cover with a cloth and let it stand 24 hours.
4. Cut the layer into small squares with a sharp knife, roll the pieces in confectioners' sugar, and put into candy paper cups. This confection will keep for weeks.

About 3 dozen pieces

Roast Chestnuts (Kastana Karvoudizmena)

4 pounds chestnuts

1. Cut a cross on the flat side of each chestnut with a small sharp knife, being careful not to damage nutmeat. Spread in a large baking pan.
2. Roast in a 425°F oven about 30 minutes, or until done; shake frequently. Serve hot.

Rusks I *(Paximathia)*

¼ cup unsalted butter
1 teaspoon vanilla extract
¾ cup sugar
3 eggs (¾ cup)
1 egg yolk
3½ cups sifted cake flour
1 tablespoon baking powder
¼ teaspoon salt
1 egg yolk for glaze

1. Beat butter and vanilla extract, then add sugar gradually, beating thoroughly. Add eggs, one at a time, beating 1 minute after each addition. Combine flour, baking powder, and salt. Add half of flour to creamed mixture and mix with a wooden spoon. Add remaining flour; mix well.
2. Divide dough into four portions. Roll each portion into a long roll about 1½ inches in diameter on a floured pastry cloth. Place rolls 3 inches apart on a well-greased and floured cookie sheet. Flatten dough slightly with hands. Brush tops with egg yolk.
3. Bake at 400°F about 20 to 25 minutes, or until golden and firm to the touch.
4. Remove from oven. Cover with a towel; let stand 2 hours.
5. Cut rolls into ½-inch slices. Place on ungreased cookie sheet, cut sides down.
6. Toast in a 400°F oven 15 to 20 minutes, turning several times until delicately brown.

About 3 dozen

Rusks II *(Paximathia)*

1 loaf Greek Easter Bread
    (Lambropsomo), page 30
Unsalted butter
Honey

1. Cut bread into thick slices. Place on ungreased cookie sheet.
2. Bake at 225°F 20 minutes on each side.
3. Cool on wire rack. Serve with butter and honey.

Rusks III *(Paximathia)*

1 cup butter
1 teaspoon vanilla extract
2 cups sugar
2 eggs
1 cup dairy sour cream
5½ cups all-purpose flour
1 teaspoon baking soda
¼ teaspoon salt

1. Cream butter, vanilla extract, and sugar. Add eggs and beat thoroughly. Stir in sour cream.
2. Mix flour, baking soda, and salt. Add to butter mixture and mix until a dough is formed.
3. Divide dough into 3 portions. Shape each portion into a roll 1½ inches in diameter. Place each roll on a cookie sheet.
4. Bake at 350°F 15 minutes. Remove from oven and turn oven control to 425°F. Using a very sharp knife, cut into ¾-inch slices. Arrange slices cut side down on cookie sheets. Bake slices first on one side, then the other, until golden brown and firm (about 6 minutes for each side). Cool on wire racks.

About 3 dozen

Sesame Seed Candy *(Pasteli)*

½ cup honey
2 cups sugar
½ cup water
3 cups sesame seed, toasted

1. Blend honey, sugar, and water in a heavy skillet. Cook over low heat, stirring frequently. Bring to a firm ball stage, 250°F on a candy thermometer (syrup will be a light gold color). Stir in sesame seed.
2. Spread in a buttered 12x8x1½-inch pan. Break into pieces.

2 to 3 dozen pieces depending on size

Koulourakia I

1 cup unsalted butter
3 eggs
2 egg yolks
2 tablespoons cognac
2 cups confectioners' sugar
4½ cups sifted cake flour
3½ teaspoons baking powder
Egg white, beaten
Sesame seed, lightly toasted

1. Beat butter until light and fluffy. Add eggs and egg yolks, one at a time, beating well after each. Add cognac, then confectioners' sugar, beating well. Sift flour with baking powder and add to butter mixture; mix well.
2. Knead dough on a floured board until shiny.
3. Break off a small amount of dough and roll on a board to form a strip 5 to 6 inches long. Shape into a ring by joining the ends, or make a snail shape by winding up the strip. Place on a greased cookie sheet. Repeat with remaining dough.
4. Brush tops with beaten egg white. Sprinkle with sesame seed.
5. Bake at 350°F 20 to 25 minutes, or until done.

About 6 dozen

Koulourakia II

3 cups sifted all-purpose flour
2 teaspoons baking powder
½ teaspoon salt
¾ cup unsalted butter
1 teaspoon anise flavoring
½ cup sugar
1 egg
¼ cup whipping cream
1 egg yolk, beaten, for brushing

1. Sift flour, baking powder, and salt together.
2. Cream butter with anise flavoring until fluffy. Add sugar and beat thoroughly. Add egg and beat well. Pour in whipping cream; mix thoroughly. Stir in flour mixture.
3. Knead dough on a floured board until shiny. Cover and refrigerate 2 hours.
4. Remove from refrigerator 30 minutes before rolling and baking. Break off a small amount of dough and roll on a board to form a strip 5 to 6 inches long. Shape into a ring by joining the ends, or make into a snail shape by winding up the strip. Place on a greased cookie sheet. Brush with egg yolk.
5. Bake at 350°F 20 to 25 minutes, or until done.

3½ dozen

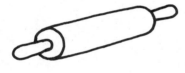

Kourambiethes

1 cup unsalted butter (at room temperature)
2 egg yolks
1 tablespoon granulated sugar
1 cup coarsely chopped blanched almonds
2 cups all-purpose flour
1 teaspoon baking powder
Whole cloves
Rosewater
2 pounds confectioners' sugar

1. Beat butter until white in an electric mixer (about 10 minutes). Add egg yolks and sugar; beat well. Add chopped almonds and mix well. Blend flour and baking powder and mix in until blended.
2. Taking a small amount of dough, roll it between palms, shaping it into a ball. Continue until all dough has been used. Or, roll dough into a round log, about 1 inch in diameter; cut diagonally into 1-inch slices. Press a clove into center of each cookie.
3. Bake at 350°F 20 minutes. Remove from oven and sprinkle lightly with rosewater. Immediately sift confectioners' sugar over them, covering the tops and sides. Cool for 1 hour.
4. Using a spatula or fork, lift the cookies, being careful not to disturb the sugar, and place them in medium-size paper cupcake cups. Store cookies at least a day before serving.

About 30 cookies

Greek Coffee *(Kafes)*

Ingredients are for one serving. To increase the servings, prepare this recipe for as many people as you wish to serve. Sugar may be increased according to taste, but it must be added before coffee is brewed. Milk is never added and the coffee is never stirred. If some guests want their coffee very sweet, or, as the Greeks say, "glykos," while others prefer theirs less sweet or "metrios," make two separate brews.

1 heaping teaspoon Greek coffee*
½ teaspoon sugar
1 demitasse cup filled almost to the brim with water

1. Place coffee and sugar in a Greek coffeepot, a briki, or a narrow saucepot. Add the water and stir until well blended.
2. Place coffee pot on low heat and wait for coffee to boil. Remove from heat. Let coffee simmer down. Return to heat. Allow to reach boiling again. Remove from heat.
3. With a spoon skim a little of the foam, called "kamaki," off the top and gently place it in the bottom of the cup. Slowly pour the coffee into the cup, being careful not to disturb the kamaki.

*Greek and Turkish coffee are the same.

CHURCH FOOD

The sacraments of Holy Communion, bread and wine, are transformed during the Divine Liturgy into the Body and Blood of Jesus Christ.

The bread used is called "Prosphoron" or "the offering." It is prepared by women parishioners according to church rules and is neither made with nor baked with any fat. After it is kneaded and shaped into a large round, it is stamped in the center with a sfragitha, a religious seal which is left on the dough while it rises. Leaving the seal on the dough insures a clear impression which is necessary because the design of the sfragitha divides it into nine squares. The center square, called the "lamb," for Jesus Christ, is embossed with the letters IC XC NIKA, an abbreviation for "Jesus Christ conquers." This is the portion that is combined with the wine for Holy Communion.

In a custom that dates back to the time of Athanasios the Great, archbishop of Alexandria in the fourth century, Kolyva, symbolizing the resurrection of Christ, is distributed after requiem services which are held on the fortieth day, at six months, and one year after a death.

The custom is in memory of the deceased, and serves as an appeal from the bereaved to the parishioners to pray for the departed soul. It derives from the Bible, John 12:24: "Verily, verily, I say until you, except a corn of wheat fall into the ground and die, it abideth alone; but if it die, it bringeth forth much fruit."

Kolyva is a combination of wheat (for the resurrection), sugar (for the sweetness of everlasting life), nuts, and spices.

At Eastertime, red eggs are the symbol of the Resurrection. The eggshell represents the tomb of Christ and the yolk and white the life held within it. The red color signifies the blood Christ shed on the cross.

Cracking these eggs is one of the most important of all the Greek customs, because breaking them signifies the opening of Christ's tomb and his conquering of death.

Easter eggs are distributed by the priest at the conclusion of the hours-long Easter services. Parishioners leaving the church greet each other with "Christos anesti" (Christ has risen) and respond with "Alythos anesti" (Truly, He has risen). Tradition dictates that they then hit each other's egg, top to top or bottom to bottom, each hoping to have the egg with the stronger shell so that it will remain unbroken. The holder of the unbroken egg then taps another and so on. It is said that the person with the last unbroken egg will have good luck and health in the coming year.

The eating of the eggs signals the end of Lent and the beginning of Easter festivities.

Church Bread *(Prosphoron)*

1 package active dry yeast
2½ cups warm water (105° to 115°F)
6 cups all-purpose flour
1 teaspoon salt
  Prosphoron seal

1. Sprinkle yeast over ¼ cup warm water; stir until dissolved.
2. Combine 5½ cups of flour and salt in a large bowl and make a well in the center. Pour in yeast and remaining warm water. Mix with a wooden spoon.
3. Sprinkle remaining flour over a board. Knead 10 minutes, adding as little flour as possible to the board. Dough will be sticky.
4. Put dough into a large bowl, cover with a cloth, and let rise in a warm place until double in bulk.
5. Sprinkle board with a little flour, punch dough down, and knead 15 minutes. (Dough should be firm and smooth.)
6. Form into a large round loaf and place in a heavily floured 12-inch round pan. Lightly flour the top of the loaf. Flour the prosphoron seal. Press seal down firmly in the center to make a sharp impression and leave on the dough.
7. Cover and allow to rise in a warm place until double in bulk. Remove seal.
8. Bake at 350°F for 1 hour. Remove from pan to cool.

Wheat for Memorial Services *(Kolyva)*

3 pounds whole wheat kernels
  Water
  Salt
3 cups sesame seed, toasted
1 pound dried golden currants
4 cups walnuts, ground
1½ cups sugar
1 tablespoon cinnamon
  Seeds from 1 or 2
    pomegranates (optional)
¾ cup flour, lightly toasted
2 pounds confectioners' sugar
½ cup silver dragées
1 pound white Jordan almonds
1 cup blanched whole almonds

1. Soak wheat kernels in water overnight. Cook in a large quantity of lightly salted water until tender, stirring frequently to prevent sticking. Drain; reserve stock for Whole Wheat Porridge with Currants and Almonds (page 86). Rinse in cold water. Drain again. Roll in dry towels until excess moisture is absorbed. Spread out on another towel to dry for several hours; stir occasionally.
2. Put wheat into a large bowl and combine with sesame seed, currants, walnuts, sugar, cinnamon, and pomegranate seeds. Toss until well mixed.
3. Line a large tray with plastic wrap or aluminum foil. Cover with white doilies. Put the Kolyva on the tray, shaping it into a mound so there will be a slight rise to the center. Press gently all over with waxed paper. Carefully sift toasted flour over Kolyva. Press down gently with waxed paper. Sift confectioners' sugar over the entire top to cover completely. Press down gently with waxed paper to form a thick, even layer over the surface.
4. Decorate the top, using two rows of white Jordan almonds to form a cross. Form the initials of the deceased with blanched almonds at the base of the cross on either side. Outline the cross and the initials with dragées. Decorate the base of Kolyva with remaining almonds and dragées.

INDEX